# TO BE A

# WOMAN

# TO BE A
# WOMAN

The Confusion Over Female Identity and How Christians Can Respond

## KATIE J. McCOY PhD

B&H
PUBLISHING
BRENTWOOD, TENNESSEE

978-1-0877-8444-1

Published by B&H Publishing Group
Brentwood, Tennessee

Dewey Decimal Classification: 305.4
Subject Heading: WOMEN \ SEX ROLE \ ANDROGYNY

Unless otherwise noted, all Scripture references are taken
from the Christian Standard Bible. Copyright © 2017
by Holman Bible Publishers. Used by permission.
Christian Standard Bible®, and CSB® are federally registered
trademarks of Holman Bible Publishers, all rights reserved.

Scripture references marked KJV are taken from
the King James Version, public domain.

Cover design by Faceout Studio, Jeff Miller.
Cover images by Reksita Wardani and White Dragon/Shutterstock.
Author photo by Katie McCoy. Color correction by Neil Williams.

1 2 3 4 5 6 • 27 26 25 24 23

To Cindy McCoy,
the first and best woman I ever met.

# Acknowledgments

I'm thankful to B&H Publishing for identifying the need to address this topic and the urgency of the moment so many followers of Christ are facing. Ashley Gorman, my editor, gave both professional guidance and personal encouragement through this process. I am grateful for her editorial expertise and her years of friendship. Mary Wiley also carved out time to read the manuscript and give helpful insights.

I cannot fail to mention the steady influence of Phil Miller, whose leadership of the Center for Church Health at Texas Baptists provides me with a focus on what matters for eternity and a freedom to pursue that in creative ways, as well as Dr. Jeff Warren, pastor of Park Cities Baptist Church, whose preaching is a model for engaging cultural issues with clarity and compassion.

And I'm thankful to the many friends who cheered me on: to Michelle, whose kingdom focus has been a sharpening presence for nearly fifteen years; to Payton, who listened with enthusiasm and curiosity to weeks' worth of research; to Tasha, whose encouraging texts always seemed to come at the right moment; and to the many who supported in countless ways—Donna, Esther, Hannah, Katie, David, Libby, Jonathan, Teresa, Ben, Sharon, Ann, and the "Minivan" Girls.

To my family: my brother, Zach, who continuously teaches me to be a better writer and an all-around better human; Dad, whose confidence is contagious and whose belief is a bolster; and Mom, without whose refining influence and vision I would never have ventured on this project or countless other endeavors. I love you all very much.

Finally, to the mothers and ministers for whom this work was written, who have shared their stories of children, patients, students, and coworkers navigating a culture of gender confusion, you have spurred and steered this research. I pray you find it increases the boldness of your witness, the depth of your compassion, and the confidence of your conviction in what it means to be a woman.

# Contents

# Cultural Chaos and Contagious Confusion

After two years of testosterone and a double mastectomy, she was still just a tired, lonely, hurt little girl. Her words.

When Heather Skribe became a Christian as a college student, she started a journey of processing the pain in her past—her parents' divorce, an abusive dad, a distant mom, and the wounding words of hearing her father say she wasn't the daughter he'd wanted. She was never a "girly girl." And her internalized sense of inadequacy evolved into self-loathing.

Heather wrestled with what the Bible said about sexuality and acknowledged her own attraction to the same sex. When she shared her struggle with a group of fellow Christians, she just needed someone to care. "Thank you for sharing that with us. . . . You're not alone—other Christians have struggled with this too. . . . Let's connect you to someone equipped to help you spiritually and emotionally. . . . You still belong here."

She didn't hear any of that.

The underlying issues of her self-perception and sexual attractions went unaddressed. Her mental health worsened after she came out as a lesbian. And again, after the high of cross-sex hormones wore off. And again, after her "top surgery." She was, in her words, "trying to modify my body to deal with soul-level heartache." Within a short span of time, she had socially, hormonally, and surgically transitioned to living as a man. Heather didn't just dislike being a woman. Heather disliked being *Heather*.

Months after her procedure, she realized her pain was beyond the reach of any surgeon. Heather sensed the Holy Spirit say to her, "Why are you settling for your brokenness? Don't you know I offer wholeness?" She may have given up on liking herself. But God hadn't given up on loving her. From that point, she began the process of detransitioning and living in harmony with the body God gave her. Today, Heather shares her story as a testimony of Jesus's power to restore and as a wake-up call to His people.

## The New Epidemic

Heather's experience is like so many others. Some 80 percent of the LGBTQ community come from a Christian or religious background. They come from your youth groups, your college Bible studies, your children's summer camps. They are in our congregations, our Christian schools or co-ops, and our families. But they are pulled between a belief system anchoring sex and gender identity in a Creator and a cultural riptide sweeping them into confusion and, in many cases, irreparable harm. If young women express disdain for their weight, shape, or skin tone, society tells them not to change themselves, but to accept who they are in the name of body positivity. The message is: *you shouldn't feel shame about your body. You should fully embrace it as it is.* But when those same young women express disdain for their biological sex, society tells them the opposite—rather than hear they should accept and embrace their bodies, they are flooded with suggestions to change themselves through medical and surgical alterations . . . all in the name of self-acceptance. Self-harm is the new self-care.[1] No wonder today's women and girls feel as though they are all at sea.

Among children and adolescents, gender dysphoria has skyrocketed in recent years, to the bewilderment and alarm of many parents. Historically, gender dysphoria nearly always afflicted boys and men. The condition typically began in early childhood (between two and four years old) and was exceedingly rare, affecting between .005 and .014 of natal males.[2] But in the last decade, the data has radically shifted. Suddenly, natal females with no history of gender confusion professed to be trans. In 2016, female-to-male (FtM) gender reassignment accounted for 46 percent of all double mastectomies. By 2017, it was 70 percent.[3] In the U.K., one of the two largest gender clinics in Europe for children and teens saw an epidemic increase in referrals over a seven-year period, from 138 cases in 2010 to more than twenty-seven hundred cases in 2019–2020. That's an increase of more than 2,000 percent in less than a decade. Also within this time frame, the average age gender transition referrals decreased, and the male-female ratio of patients shifted in favor of natal females. Among eleven- to seventeen-year-olds, four hundred of the five hundred referrals for gender transition were girls. That's more than 75 percent.[4] In 2007, the U.S. had only one gender clinic for adolescents. By 2021, that number jumped to at least fifty.[5] In other words, gender confusion is not just growing, it's erupting, and by a landslide, it's *girls* who seem to be most affected by the explosion.

Gender ideology is also influencing children at progressively younger ages. Before they can register to vote, drive a car, recite their multiplication tables, or even form a complete sentence, parents and health-care providers are facilitating, and at times imposing, social transition. Outlets like Healthychildren.org, the official parenting website of the American Academy of Pediatrics, claims children have a "stable sense of their gender identity" by the age of four.[6] Boston Children's Hospital claims toddlers are cognizant of their trans-identity and communicate it by playing with cross-gender toys and refusing haircuts.[7] The top-rated pediatric research hospital also features a gynecologist explaining the concept of gender-affirming hysterectomies.[8] And for a medical center trying to boost its bottom line, "gender-affirming surgeries" are big business. In 2022, a recording of Vanderbilt University's Medical Center physician, Shayne Taylor, circulated in which the doctor described just how lucrative "top surgeries" on minors promised to be. "Huge money-makers," she called them.[9]

One prominent gender therapist in San Francisco claims children know their gender identity as young as three years old. Diane Ehrensaft, author of *The Gender Creative Child*, says children may send preverbal "gender messages" to parents communicating their true gender. A male toddler who unsnaps his onesie is creating a dress to identify as a girl. A female toddler may state, "I boy!" and persistently resist wearing barrettes and hair bows to identity as a boy.[10] All this long before the child's prefrontal cortex—the part of the brain responsible for proper evaluation of a situation, decision making, and emotional impulse control—is developed. In a closed Facebook group for parents who identify and affirm their child's transgender identity, moms and dads trade tips on how to socially present their little ones as the opposite gender, including how to tuck in shirts to flatten genitals for their "daughter" and where to purchase a crocheted prosthetic penis and testicles for their "son."[11] These parents believe they are giving support, acceptance, and love. They believe they are granting the freedom of unrestrained, uninfluenced self-determination. And this self-determination has no limits.

The last decade has also witnessed a surge in gender variants. In 2014, Facebook announced fifty-eight gender options by which users could identify themselves.[12] Other sources claim the number of genders is more than seventy.[13] And it seems to be an ever-expanding social category. One can identify as *ambigender*, having "two specific gender identities simultaneously without any fluidity or fluctuations"; *demigender*, having "partial traits of one gender and the rest of the other gender," or *femfluid*, "fluctuating regarding the feminine genders." There is *angenital* identity, in which a person doesn't want any sexual characteristics but still retains a gender; *omnigender*, in which one has or experiences all genders, and *blankgirl*, in which a girl can't describe her womanhood as anything more than a "blank space."[14] Most recently, gender has become blurred with other species, such as *xenogender*, where someone's gender identity can't be contained by human categories and is expressed by relating to animals or plants, and more specifically "*catgirl*," a gender identity associated with cats and feeling feline.[15] These stated identities are admittedly rare. However, the logic behind them is consistent. If gender identity is disconnected from and unrelated to biological sex, then people are free to craft their identities according to their attitudes and affinities. Gender becomes a transient feeling, an ephemeral impression that can change over the course of one's life, even one's day.

The dominant cultural narrative claims gender nonconforming identities are a significant portion of our society. Coming out as trans or nonbinary has become in vogue among celebrities, including Halsey, Cara Delevingne, Ellen/Elliot Page, Demi Lovato, and Janelle Monae. Publications marketed to adolescent and young women like *Teen Vogue* and *Cosmopolitan* frequently feature content related to trans and nonbinary culture. The trend has, predictably, reached its market, as middle and high school students report gender nonconformity among their peers as increasingly prevalent.

Addressing the gender narrative is daunting enough, but on top of that, its counternarrative is systematically silenced. In a society where views are "violence" and words are "weapons," any speech that questions, much less opposes, the prevailing gender narrative is considered dangerous, harmful, a threat to civil rights, and "unsafe." When a United States senator pressed a Berkeley law professor about whether men could get pregnant, she accused him of transphobia and contributing to violence against, and the suicidality of, transgender people.[16] Depending on the news outlets or social media platforms you frequent, you may never have heard of scholars and authors producing well-researched responses to gender ideology. Various retail outlets removed books like Debra Soh's *The End of Gender*, Ryan Anderson's *When Harry Became Sally*, and Abigail Shreir's *Irreversible Damage* after receiving complaints about their content. When the American Booksellers Association sent *Irreversible Damage* to its vendors, it later issued an apology for committing a "serious, violent incident" that went against their policies, values, and everything they believe and support.[17] Dare to claim openly that only females can be women and risk being plunged into social media purgatory and professional demise.[18] Anything less than unqualified affirmation and agreement is typically treated as transphobia. Disagreement, however peaceably conveyed, has become synonymous with hate.

## What We're Doing Here

In high school, my favorite class was Mr. Eaton's "Intro to Journalism." And not just because we got to watch *All the President's Men*. Mr. Eaton instilled a love for asking good questions, for digging deeper. And like any good journalism teacher, he instilled the rudiments of good reporting: asking *who, what, where, when, why,* and *how.*

As we sift through the confusion over female identity, we'll consider five different spheres that shape and form our view. At points, these spheres overlap. At other times, they exclude one another. But at every point, they influence the formation of female identity.

**Who:** This is the *theological* sphere. It is the foundation of our identity. Who we are answers what it means to be human, specifically to be a woman.

**What:** This is the *biological* sphere. It describes the complexity of femaleness and the essential, verifiable differences between male and female.

**Where:** This is the *relational* sphere. It is the arena in which one's gender identity is expressed and confirmed by others.

**Why:** This is the *philosophical* sphere. It explains the cultural chaos we see surrounding sex and gender. Turns out, the ideas that have produced our new understanding of identity are not new at all.

**How:** This is the *social* sphere. It represents the means by which the confusion over female identity has become main-stream and considered a moral good.

(If you're wondering where that fifth "w" is—*when*—well, you answered that one when you picked up this book. It's right now!)

Ordinarily, I'd begin with the theological sphere and build on biblical revelation. God's Word is, after all, the foundation of our identity as human beings. It reveals our nature, diagnoses our condition, and gives hope for real life-change. But on this topic, I'd like to approach things a little differently. Let's start with what we see and work backwards.

We'll begin with the social factor, which includes some of the most obvious evidence for *how* female identity has become so confused. Then, we'll consider *why*, analyzing the philosophical ideas that have justified the social confusion we see. The way we relate to one another is the sphere *where* we articulate or convey our philosophy of humanity, sex, and gender. But, despite the social, philosophical, and relational factors and the influence they wield, we cannot erase the biological facts of femaleness. *What* we are is fundamentally complex and cannot be changed. Finally, we consider *who* we are as human beings created by God. This provides the framework through which we understand every other factor and its influence on our identity.

With these factors in mind, here is the main idea of this book:

> *Female identity is socially guided, philosophi-cally formed, relationally confirmed, biologically grounded, and theologically bestowed.*

Now, I'm not a counselor, a psychologist, or a medical doctor. But I've done my best to present the leading voices of experts and scholars on the different aspects of this question. They include psychologists, neurobiologists, pediatricians, sociologists, gender theorists, and other theologians. Before venturing further, you should know my own frame of reference. I'll be building on three important presuppositions:

First, I hold to a Christian worldview. I believe the Bible is God's revelation of Himself and that what it says about male and female, gender, sexuality, sin, redemption, and everything else is true. And if you've come to this book outside of that worldview and this offends you, making you want to shut this book and assume the worst, I get it. But before you do, consider that we all have a worldview. It's our framework for answering the core questions of life: Where did we come from? What went wrong? and How do we fix it? How you answer those questions will reveal your worldview. A Christian worldview answers those questions according to the Bible and the historic teachings of the Christian faith or, more specifically, this way: *creation, fall, redemption,* and *restoration.*

Second, I believe a woman is an adult human female and a girl is a prepubescent human female. As I state these things, please know I don't intend to be inflammatory. But in a culture that anchors reality in personal feelings over (and against) empirical facts, claiming males can't be women is often considered intractably intolerant and perilously transphobic.

Third, I believe gender dysphoria is a psychological condition, one that deserves compassion and expert care to treat and overcome. When someone experiences gender incongruence, in which one's biological sex and self-perception of gender are misaligned, the condition is a matter of the mind, not the body.

In his book *Embodied*, Preston Sprinkle articulates this, saying our biological sex "determines who we are . . . and our embodiment is an essential part of how we image God in the world."[19] Some people experience a mental condition called *body integrity dysphoria*, meaning they feel one or more of their limbs don't align with what their bodies should be. One might believe, for example, her own arm or leg is somehow foreign to her body. It doesn't feel like *her* limb, even though physical reality communicates that it is. Said another way, her self-perception doesn't match physical reality. In light of this, she may request a doctor to amputate a healthy, functioning limb. For someone with this condition, a doctor would (hopefully) not amputate a perfectly healthy limb, but rather try to help the patient become at ease with her body, the goal being to realign her self-perception with physical reality. The same logic should apply to those with gender dysphoria: the goal should be to help her accept her body and no longer want to alter her outer self to fit her inner self.

Throughout this book, I'll refer to the dominant cultural paradigm of sex and gender identity as "gender ideology." In some ways, it's a catchall phrase to reflect the theories, claims, and aims of our society's prevailing view of gender. But at its core, gender ideology rests on the belief that one's biological category (i.e., the sexed body) is divisible from one's personal identity (i.e., the gendered self), that the physical you and the real you are mutually exclusive. How and why this approach to gender has become the dominant mindset, we'll unpack throughout the rest of the chapters.

I'll also use the terms *transgender, trans,* and at times *nonbinary* to reflect various identities within gender ideology. For example, a person who identifies as *demigender* may not think of herself as transgender, but *transgender* is the umbrella term to include identities in which one's sense of gender does not correspond to one's biology. You may want to review the glossary of terms I'll be using throughout for their definitions. Wherever possible, I'll employ terms and phrases as you will encounter them culturally.

## Individuals or Issues?

Five years after she began to detransition from identifying as a man, Keira experienced a sign that she was becoming herself again: she could cry. When she was flooded with testosterone, she—like many other trans men—had found herself unable to release her emotions. She had a lot to cry about.

Before she was legally an adult, Keira had endured overwhelming setbacks. Her parents divorced when she was young. Her mother was an alcoholic with mental illness. Her father was distant. She was a tomboy who preferred playing sports with the boys in school. Upon the onset of puberty, she found herself attracted to other girls and wondered what was wrong with her. Her mom asked her if she was a boy, which sent her into a downward spiral of gender confusion.

When she was referred to the Gender Identity Development Service clinic in London, she insisted she needed to transition. "It was the kind of brash assertion that's typical of teenagers," she shares. "What was really going on was that I was a girl insecure in my body who had experienced parental abandonment, felt alienated from my peers, suffered from anxiety and depression, and struggled with my sexual orientation." A few surface-level conversations later, doctors granted Keira her wish, without ever addressing the issues behind her gender dysphoria. I wish her experiences were rare. A generation of girls are manifesting their pain through transgender identities, while those charged with their care neglect the sources of their mental suffering.

As we consider the beliefs and practices within gender ideology, we must never forget the human beings affected by it. Despite our culture's unmatched acceptance of gender nonconformity and support for gender transition, suicide rates continue to rise.[20] The "cures" are causing greater harm. Gender ideology exploits their vulnerability and calls it health care.

Behind these headlines are real people. Confused and wounded people who need spiritual and psychological care. Gender dysphoria is a genuine condition in which someone feels as though she's been born in the wrong body. It includes acute, psychological distress, sometimes inducing tendencies to self-harm or suicide. It is a complex condition and is often rooted in deep-seated pain and misguided beliefs about one's gender. People with gender dysphoria often feel isolated and alienated. Like many internal afflictions, gender dysphoria can also induce physical symptoms. One gender dysphoric person described the feeling as "an electric current" that makes for aching joints and a turning stomach. Another described it as a "numb but painful" feeling throughout the body. "Painful."[21] "Not being able to feel at home in your own body."[22]

Sprinkle describes two trends in transgender conversation. Some people only see a "culture war," expressing outrage over the illogic of what they see and hear on the news. They see an issue but can't possibly know there are people around them struggling with the very thing they view as a punch line of a joke or fodder for memes. Others only see people's need for love, ignoring the theological and scientific facts about sex and gender. They see people but empathize without critical thought and offer little hope of healing or life-change. I'm convinced we'll find a balance between these two extremes individually when we are a witness corporately. In the balance of truth and love, most of us tend to lean more toward one over the other. (Yet another reason we need the *whole* body of Christ—the theologian and the ethicist, and the counselor and the psychologist, the teacher and the mother—to speak into this issue with their respective gifts, expertise, and perspectives.) How much more effective might we be if we emphasized how we can learn from one another more than how we differ from one another?

## Conclusion

In Jesus's time, being sick or disabled came with stigma and shame. You may have been forbidden from going into the temple, which conveyed the ceremonial purity God required of His people to approach Him. In many cases, you'd be prevented from working, marrying, or having a family, which was essential for social relationships and economic security in an ancient, agrarian society. You were an outsider, marginalized, cut off from the community. In an honor/shame culture like the Bible's, this was devastating.

Jesus dropped everything when He met people with these kinds of needs. He broke religious traditions and drew the ire of the social elite in order to help them. To be physically healed meant more than recovery from a condition. It meant being restored to a community. Those whom Jesus restored didn't remain marginalized. They were brought from isolation to connection. From alienation to acceptance.

The affliction of gender confusion or dysphoria may not be outwardly visible. But overwhelmingly, the women and girls who suffer from it feel every bit as alienated—not only from others but also from themselves. Were Jesus walking among us today, I can't help but wonder how He would respond to the lonely little girl who feels like she doesn't fit or to the broken woman trying to heal herself of a soul-deep wound.

He would be as He always has been—infinitely kind, tender-hearted, patient, understanding, and deeply moved by her pain. And, He would love her enough to tell her the truth in a spirit of gentleness and grace.

We are His ambassadors, His messengers entrusted with good news: they don't have to settle for their brokenness. He offers them wholeness. He gave His own body to recover and restore those who feel alienated from their own bodies. Better still, He brings them into the body of Christ.

# CHAPTER 1

# How: The Formative Effect of Social Influence

B y the time she could drive, Chloe had already received puberty blockers, testosterone, a double mastectomy, and a lifetime of regret.[1] She's among the countless young women who were rushed into gender transitions. Women who obtained treatments that failed to take away their dysphoria. Women whose procedures left scars far deeper than their postoperative wounds.

As we discovered in the introduction, until recently, gender dysphoria was a rare occurrence predominantly found among young boys, some of them as young as two to four years old when symptoms of early-onset gender dysphoria appeared.[2] Yet, seemingly overnight, those statistics dramatically shifted. The last ten to fifteen years have witnessed a surge in "late-onset gender dysphoria," a condition occurring among adolescents and young adults, 70 percent of whom are girls.[3]

In this chapter, we explore how this phenomenon came to be. We'll consider the therapeutic methods, the hormonal and surgical treatments, and the underlying issues influencing so many adolescent and young women to embrace transgender identity. These topics are complex—condensing a world of trends, theories, and therapies to a few pages would test the brevity of a Haiku poet. But, through all the data points and discussions, we can conclude one thing: female identify is, undeniably, socially formed. The question is, Who or what is forming it?

## The Rise of ROGD (Rapid-Onset Gender Dysphoria)

When physician-scientist, Lisa Littman, explored why so many adolescent and young adults suddenly identified as transgender, she couldn't have predicted the responses she would receive, either from the parents she interviewed or the public she informed.

The Brown University professor received survey responses from more than 250 parents whose adolescent and young adult children, although previously expressing no gender incongruence before middle or high school, came out as trans. Most agreed their child's announcement of trans identity came out of nowhere. Within weeks, teenage girls went from no expression of gender dysphoria to claiming they were transgender and wanting to medically transition.[4]

The average age of the represented children was sixteen. More than 80 percent of them were natal females. Littman coined this trend, which overwhelmingly occurred among adolescent girls, "Rapid Onset Gender Dysphoria" (ROGD). Her research found three key connections between adolescents and

ROGD: first, the influence of the girl's friend group; second, the tendency to manifest gender dysphoria as a coping mechanism for other issues; and third, increased social media consumption.[5]

Littman called the sharp increase in trans-identified girls a "social contagion." A social contagion is the spread of certain behaviors, attitudes, or feelings, similar to a virus. People who are vulnerable to a social contagion have "heightened suggestibility," meaning they're likely to accept the suggested actions of other people.[6] Want a perfect example of suggestibility? Imagine I just yawned, . . . and I mean one of those big, deep, right-before-falling-asleep yawns that signals to your brain that it's time to float off to dreamland. Did you just yawn too? (I've yawned twice since typing that.)

Girls with ROGD are influenced by a type of social contagion, one that comes from peers who mutually influence one another to promote negative emotions and behaviors. Eating disorders and bullying are two common peer contagions. So are symptoms of depression and repeatedly discussing problems or "co-ruminating" over emotions. (As in, what most teenage girls incessantly do.[7])

Littman compared the spread of ROGD to the spread of anorexia among adolescents and young adults. In both cases, girls internalize symptoms and behaviors together. Anorexic teens chronically talk about their weight, their body image, and their weight loss techniques. They admire other anorexics whose devotion to resisting weight gain creates physical complications. They ridicule anorexics who submit to therapy and medical treatment. Anorexic peers even coach one another on how to deceive parents and physicians. And they invest time online at niche websites that reinforce these attitudes and actions.

The peer contagion theory may explain why the male-female ratio of gender dysphoria reversed so drastically in such a short time frame. It also connects to what we already know about how females think, feel, and behave. They are wired for connection, identification, and harmony in their relationships. In some cases, girls will suspend reality to affirm what their friends do just so they can preserve the friendship.[8] Among parents Littman surveyed, over one-third reported that the majority of the members in their child's friend-group identified as transgender. One fourteen-year-old girl and her three friends were close to a popular coach who had announced a trans identity. Within a year, all four of the teens announced the same.

Social media consumption also played a major role in adolescents and young adults with ROGD. Websites like YouTube, Reddit, TikTok, and Tumblr are like convoluted rabbit holes of suggestion and circular reasoning. Teens find online communities and social media influencers sharing the euphoria they felt after transitioning and why it's urgent viewers pursue transition without delay, along with the freedom from hating their bodies they found through hormone therapies and operations.[9] Vague feelings, so common to adolescent life, are said to confirm life-long, unrealized gender nonconformity.

Finally, the *coup de grâce* of online advice: if you're asking whether you're trans, you probably are. It took me all of fifteen seconds on Reddit to stumble upon The Gender Bible, a website devoted to navigating gender dysphoria.[10] The section titled, "Am I Trans?" validates gender-questioning readers with statements like, "Most cis people don't think about their gender very much," so if you get "energy" from the idea of yourself as a different gender, that probably means something. Feeling sad or odd indicates an undiscovered trans identity, because most cisgender people "actively like" being the gender they were assigned at birth. Typical teen angst—or even just feeling the unpleasant emotions that come with a bad day—translates to closeted trans identity.

Trans influencers even coach adolescents on what to tell parents and therapists, specific words or phrases to guarantee hormone treatments after their first visit to a clinic. Parents picked up on the language their children used and how different it was from their own voice. Many suspected it sounded like something they'd heard or read online. They were right. The verbiage in their child's announcement was "verbatim," "word-for-word," or "practically copy and paste" from online sources. The words and phrases of trans influencers became part of a script.

Another sociological element to ROGD connects with one of current society's most prevalent ideas. The majority of adolescent girls who suddenly come out as trans are white and middle class. Researchers believe they know why: in a culture where your credibility is linked to your victim status, being a white, middle-class girl isn't "special."[11] The only intersectional identity you can choose is trans identity. A seventeen-year-old described how she was exposed to LGBT content and activism on Instagram when she was eleven and noticed the affirmation trans people received: "I saw how trans people online got an overwhelming amount of support, and the amount of praise they were getting really spoke to me because, at the time, I didn't really have a lot of friends of my own." Once a girl says she's transgender, she's met with positive attention and social approval. She now represents an oppressed segment of society. Her voice—indeed, her life—now has meaning beyond herself as she decries "white male privilege," "straight privilege," and other evidence of her own victimhood.[12] One young woman shared how, as a teenager, she felt political pressure to transition, describing the trans activist community as "very social justice-y": "There was a lot of negativity around being a cis, heterosexual, white girl, and I took those messages really, really personally."[13] In a society where oppression and marginalization increasingly equal status and credibility, and where race and gender predict the validity of your voice, trans identity becomes an appealing social distinction.

Littman's study also found a connection between ROGD and other mental health issues. Many of the adolescents and young adults represented in her survey had past trauma, self-harming behaviors, or difficulty coping with negative emotions. Prior to announcing their trans identity, an overwhelming number of girls had been diagnosed with a psychiatric disorder within the last one to two years. Over two-thirds had social anxiety in their teens, and more than 40 percent tended to isolate themselves from peers or have trouble interacting with them. While we should be clear that trauma isn't a catchall cause of ROGD, we also shouldn't miss the fact that it plays a significant role. Nearly half had experienced a traumatic event shortly before their ROGD, such as a parent's divorce or death, rape or attempted rape, sexual harassment, an abusive romantic relationship, a breakup, bullying, isolation, changing schools, serious illness, or hospitalization. A twelve-year-old girl was bullied when she started puberty earlier than other girls. She said she hated her breasts. Websites told her hating your breasts indicated trans identity. A sixteen-year-old girl was traumatized by a sexual assault. Months after the rape, she announced she was transgender. For her, ROGD was a coping mechanism.

Psychologists have a name for this phenomenon: psychic epidemics. People convince themselves they have an ailment then manifest the symptoms. Psychoanalyst Dr. Lisa Marchiano explained how it occurs: when we are psychologically troubled, we look for ways to explain it so we will receive the concern and care we need. A "prescribed narrative" gives us something to latch onto, a way to communicate our mental and emotional problems. People gravitate to culturally acceptable ways of expressing their internal distress, called "symptom pools." When a few highly publicized cases receive attention, patients may start to identify with the symptoms as a way to communicate their own pain. Soon those symptoms catch on and become the "new social script." In Marchiano's view, gender dysphoria has become the new symptom pool.[14]

Abigail Favale states the same concept from a different angle. Our culture has built a structure for trans people to interpret and categorize their experiences of gender incongruence. But trans-identifying people didn't develop the framework; the framework developed them: "[T]he development of that framework has led to transgender identification. There are people in turmoil, and the gender paradigm has become the dominant lens for interpreting that turmoil."[15]

To be clear, the psychological distress is genuine. The anguish is genuine. Even psychologists who believe the gender dysphoria craze is a social contagion or psychic epidemic acknowledge the reality of the mental suffering that's driving it.[16] The last thing a Christian needs to do with all this information is act like the underlying mental and emotional health issues behind all of this aren't real. They are. After all, we live in a fallen world that affects not just to our relationship with God, but our relationship with others and even with our own selves, body, mind, and soul. These issues should be treated with tender compassion and informed care. But, overwhelmingly, for the majority of girls coming out as trans, gender dysphoria isn't the primary issue. While gender dysphoria may be the underlying issue for a small fraction of those who struggle with gender confusion, *it is not for most.*

Instead, for most girls identifying as trans, it's a way to focus on their unhappiness and cope with their problems.[17] These girls aren't acting. They're redirecting.

And the "help" they receive is doing even more harm.

## The New Standard of Care

The "prevailing standard of care" for treating gender dysphoria is called *affirmative therapy* or *gender-affirming care*. Affirmative therapy practitioners affirm the patient's self-diagnosis of gender dysphoria and self-assessment of gender identity. A therapist not only agrees that the female patient *feels like* a boy trapped in a girl's body, or *wants* to become and live as a boy, but that the female patient really *is* a boy.[18] Affirmative therapy is submitting your perspective to the patient's perspective: she has the best understanding of her own gender; only she knows what her identity really is. The therapist's role is not to question the teenager's stated gender identity but to "follow the child's lead,"[19] and "facilitate the patient's range of options."[20] In the words of Dr. Colton Wasserman, associate medical director for Planned Parenthood: "It's vital for trans people, especially young trans people, to access the supportive, affirming health care *they* choose." Though the patient is going to a doctor whose specialty is to diagnose and treat, the patient diagnoses herself, determines her gender identity, then recommends her own treatment.

The textbook, *A Clinician's Guide to Gender-Affirming Care*, describes affirmative therapy as client centered: "Self-determination and autonomy are seen as key in providing affirming care . . . clients have the right to say who they are."[21] Therapists help clients "unlearn" social expressions and phrases such as referring to people as "men and women," rather than "people of all genders."[22]

Affirmative therapy goes beyond compassion, sensitivity, and attunement. We would hope any good therapist would have these for his or her patients. But we would also hope a counselor would challenge flawed ideas and discover underlying issues. For what other psychiatric condition does treatment focus on automatically agreeing with the patient, then altering physical reality to fit her self-perception?[23]

Nearly every medical or professional organization endorses affirmative therapy as the only proper response to someone's stated gender. The American Academy of Pediatrics (AAP) recommends "gender-affirming," nonjudgmental care for gender-diverse children and adolescents.[24] The American Psychological Association (APA) states they "continuously learn more . . . about helping our children discover and fortify their true gender selves."[25] They encourage doctors to "adapt or modify their understanding of gender" to have a broader range of what they consider "healthy and normative."[26] And the World Professional Association for Transgender Health includes affirming gender identity and exploring options to express that identity in its document, "Standards of Care."[27]

Affirmative therapy rests on the belief that adolescents have a stable sense of gender identity.[28] But no long-term studies can confirm this claim.[29] In fact, data demonstrates that the very stage of human development most clarifying for a girl's gender identity is what gender-affirming care manipulates and prevents. It also implies that four out of five gender dysphoric children and teens are undergoing treatments they wouldn't otherwise want.

Until recently, mental health professionals approached gender-dysphoric children with "watchful waiting." Watchful waiting neither encouraged nor discouraged a child's stated gender. Instead, doctors would wait to observe whether the dysphoria would persist or desist as the child matured both emotionally and mentally. Watchful waiting also looked at other factors that may have been influencing the patient's self-perception or views of gender. It considered the whole child.[30]

The method was incredibly effective. Most children with early-onset gender dysphoria (pre- and elementary-school ages) grew to identify with their biological sex after going through puberty. This isn't a statistical gamble, either. The rate of desistence is somewhere between 80 percent and 90 percent. While some trans activists dismiss the data as "junk science,"[31] at least a dozen studies confirm what London's Gender Identity Development Service found: "90.3 percent of young people who did not commence [puberty blockers] desisted."[32]

Thus, Dr. Kenneth Zucker, clinical psychologist and former head of the Toronto Gender Clinic, is a proponent of watchful waiting in children. Zucker believes any form of gender transition—social, hormonal, or surgical—just reinforces the gender dysphoria at a stage when the child is learning behavior that harmonizes with his or her biological sex.[33] With therapy to address the underlying cause of the child's dysphoria, and with no social or medical interference, most gender-dysphoric children will no longer identify with the opposite gender.[34] If, that is, they aren't encouraged to transition.[35]

That's a big "if."

Today, any approach other than gender-affirmative care is condemned as "conversion therapy." For decades, conversion therapy referred to attempts to change or "cure" someone's same-sex attractions to a heterosexual preference. It's an approach many orthodox Christians have denounced, believing a person can live a chaste, God-honoring life even if their same-sex attraction never goes away. But that's not how proponents of affirmative therapy define it. Instead, any attempt to align gender identity with biological sex is branded as harmful, cruel, regressive "conversion therapy."

In 2015, Dr. Zucker discovered just how ruthless affirmative therapy proponents can be. Zucker's career centered on treating gender-dysphoric patients. He spearheaded the written entry on gender dysphoria in the *Diagnostic and Statistical Manual*, 5th edition (DSM-5) and helped author the "Standards of Care" guidelines for the World Professional Association for Transgender Health.[36] While he wasn't opposed to gender transition, he used caution with patients under eighteen and believed they shouldn't be rushed into hormonal or surgical therapies. Zucker focused on "treating the whole kid" and had great success with his young patients. Despite his reputation as an international authority on the topic, gender activists decried his "watchful waiting" practice, accused his methods of being unhealthy for trans children and teens, and lobbied Zucker's organization until they took disciplinary action against him. Zucker was fired from his Toronto clinic. No matter how decorated and storied the career, a mental health professional who fails to adopt affirmative therapy is liable to be "canceled."

The medical community claims children should be allowed to get treatments and therapies if their dysphoria is "consistent, persistent, and insistent."[37] But what if the medical community is facilitating, if not manifesting, these criteria among impressionable young women and girls?

## Behind the Surge of ROGD

Grace battled depression as a young twentysomething. After years of "obsessing" over her identity, she developed gender dysphoria.[38] The idea of medically becoming and living as a man made her euphoric. She finally felt a glimmer of hope. Grace had everything she needed—access to hormonal treatments, health insurance to facilitate her transition, and a supportive network of relationships. What she didn't have was a therapist who would help her examine the underlying issues she had before she started her hormonal and surgical transition. "Instead," she describes, "I was diagnosed with gender dysphoria and given the green light to start transition by my doctor on the first visit."

Grace began with cross-sex hormone injections and, four months later, had a double mastectomy. She wept for joy when her treatments began. A year later, she wept with remorse, full of grief as she clutched her double-mastectomy scars. "My gender dysphoria, which I had taken as proof that I was truly meant to live as male, turned out to stem from other mental health issues. My change had been a brutal mistake, and I would have to live with the consequences—numb scars, no breasts, a deepened voice—for the rest of my life." Grace was left to diagnose herself, then left to wonder why a therapist didn't help her diagnose what was driving her dysphoria.

Today, Grace is among the growing ranks of "detransition-ers," people who formerly identified as transgender and, to varying degrees, undertook a gender transition. As the president of Gender Care Consumer Advocacy Network, she's raising awareness about the lack of responsible and safe medical care the trans community receives.

Her experience is becoming common. Girls with ROGD have mental health problems that go unexplored and untreated.

Even children with early-onset gender dysphoria may be expressing an issue that has little to do with gender confusion. One little boy thought girls were treated nicer in school. To his child's mind, maybe if he were a girl, his teacher wouldn't yell at him as much.[39] A little girl wanted to be a boy after she witnessed her mother being physically abused. To her child's mind, being a girl like mommy meant the world was a more dangerous place. Some children perceive the parental disdain of being the opposite gender than what their mother or father wanted. To their child's mind, if they were different, maybe mommy or daddy would love them.[40] Other children confuse gender identity with surface expressions of gendered behaviors. Zucker describes how a seven-year-old boy said he wanted to be a girl because he didn't like to sweat and only boys sweat. These are innocent children that need nurture and guidance, not hormones and surgeries.

Researchers have also identified a connection between gender dysphoria and autism, since those on the autism spectrum are overrepresented among gender-dysphoric children.[41] A Canadian mom, Victoria G., shared her experience with a gender clinic.[42] She suspected her teenage daughter, Jane, was on the autism spectrum, which may have contributed to her depressive symptoms. Shortly after seeing a therapist, Jane wanted cross-sex hormones and a double mastectomy. Victoria's health insurance plan gave easy and inexpensive access to both testosterone injections and an elective mastectomy but no coverage for psychological or therapeutic care. Think about that. It was easier—and cheaper—to obtain irreversible hormonal and surgical treatment for gender dysphoria than it was to discover and treat the root causes of the dysphoria. Victoria reflects on how she naïvely assumed her daughter would receive a "comprehensive psychological assessment with therapy" before being introduced to gender-altering treatments. She claims affirmative care is ultimately harmful: "Parents have the right to know what type of treatment and assessment their child will really receive." Victoria's intuition about Jane was correct: autism spectrum disorder coupled with polycystic ovary syndrome had manifested as gender dysphoria. Jane's dysphoria was genuine and had an identifiable cause. But her gender therapist only addressed Jane's symptoms. Worse than that, the gender therapist *adapted* to Jane's symptoms. What was happening is the equivalent of prescribing a fourth-grader Tylenol every day for headaches and insisting she sit in the front row at school but refusing to have her eyes checked. As it turns out, when the root causes of Jane's distress were treated, her gender dysphoria eventually resolved.[43]

Finally, we cannot ignore the significant link between gender dysphoria and sexual abuse.[44] While every case can't be blamed on abuse, I've lost count of how many stories I've read about young women whose rapid-onset gender dysphoria was a form of psychological survival. Women like Erin Brewer, who, along with her brother, was abducted by two men when she was six years old. She was brutally sexually assaulted, but her brother was not. To her child's mind, if she'd been a boy, those men wouldn't have hurt her. Shortly after the assault, Erin said she was a boy. She would put duct tape over her vagina to hide it and wear her brother's clothes.[45]

In her children's book, *Always Erin,* she shares how she learned to talk about her feelings and realized that being a boy wouldn't stop her from being hurt again. Erin shares how thankful she is not to have grown up in today's culture, where parents and teachers would almost certainly have interpreted her actions as gender-based rather than trauma-based. Gradually, with regular therapy, Erin realized no matter how much she wanted to be a boy, she was a girl.[46] After decades of self-destructive actions, Erin encountered Jesus Christ, and her life was radically changed. Today, she shares her story and warns of the dangers of gender ideology.[47] Were Erin a child in today's society, she would have received gender-reassignment treatments but might never get help to address the violent violation her gender dysphoria expressed: "I will be forever grateful for therapists who helped me understand that my gender dysphoria was a coping mechanism that my creative mind came up with to help me make sense of my trauma."

These stories reinforce Littman's hypothesis that social influences contribute to gender dysphoria among teen girls. ROGD is often an inadequate coping mechanism that delays or avoids treatment for underlying mental health problems. It also alienates patients from their parents and other social support systems. Gender transition becomes, in Littman's words, "intentional self-harm."[48]

It's unfathomable to me how any therapist, counselor, or psychiatrist worthy of the profession could fail to at least inquire about, much less identify, any potential underlying cause of gender dysphoria, how they would facilitate a coping mechanism that only further suppresses the root problems and creates irreversible damage. But the harm affirmative care practitioners are causing doesn't end there.

## But Won't They Commit Suicide?

The question has immobilized countless parents with uncertainty and fear: "Would you rather have a dead daughter or a living son?" Pediatricians, psychologists, and gender therapists present two options: either affirm your child's gender identity or give her over to depression, anxiety, suicidality, and possible self-harm.[49] What parent wouldn't move heaven and earth and do whatever was necessary to save their child? The rate of suicide attempts among trans people is heart-stopping. We cannot look away from that, especially as Christians who believe in the sacredness of life. At the same time, we cannot look away from the fact that many therapists (and social media influencers) reveal that the threat of suicide is being weaponized against parents' concerns, convictions, and even common sense.

Dr. Marcus Evans describes how gender therapists and psychologists make terrified parents feel that any expression of hesitance or skepticism, or simple deliberation before making a drastic move, is a recipe for suicide.[50] Trans-identified teens have even been encouraged by social media and members of the transgender community to threaten suicide if their parents resist their medical transition. One gender therapist advises them to fake a suicide attempt so they're taken seriously: "Pull a stunt. Suicide every time. They will give you want you need."[51] Fearing their child will harm herself if she is denied treatment, mothers and fathers are rushed into approving major medical interventions, a pattern doctors like Evans describe as manipulative, or "emotional terrorism."[52] Despite their reservations and concerns, they consented to hormonal and surgical treatments that changed their child's life irrevocably.

Suicide attempts among gender-dysphoric people are staggeringly high. And for a generation of girls declaring themselves trans, it's a chronic, top-of-mind fear. Especially when medical professionals talk about suicide statistics.

A 2014 study conducted by the Williams Institute claimed 41 percent of transgender and gender-nonconforming adults attempted suicide.[53] It's an overwhelming number and one that is referenced early and often in a child's gender journey. The perception that transgender people are one crisis away from the brink of suicide has practically made its way into our social consciousness.

But it's not the whole story.

The same study also found that the largest group to report a suicide attempt (60 percent of those surveyed) also suffered from a mental health issue. But the research didn't explore mental health status and history, despite those being "important risk factors for both attempted and completed suicide in the general population." Its authors also admit the number may be inflated since they didn't ask any clarifying or follow-up questions. For instance, respondents weren't asked when the suicide attempt took place: Was it before or after they sought or received a gender transition? Was the suicide attempt caused by their gender dysphoria or by another mental health problem?[54] That's essential information to know. Because, for many trans and gender-nonconforming people, hormonal and surgical treatment only made things worse. Much worse.

A 2011 Swedish study strongly implied "poor psychological outcomes" for those who transitioned. Unlike the 2014 study, this one adjusted the figures to consider prior psychiatric illnesses. It didn't skew the numbers. They found that, among *postoperative transsexuals*, suicide attempts were five times more likely, and hospitalization for psychiatric care was three times more likely. Even more harrowing, people who transitioned were *nineteen times more likely to commit suicide.*

We don't know whether gender transition treatments and surgeries *caused* the increase in suicides or *correlated* to other factors contributing to it.[55] But we do know the effects of affirmative therapy do not deliver the relief, much less the remedy, for gender dysphoria the psychiatric community so widely claims.

If this were any other issue, the medical community would sound a collective outcry. They would demand that all procedures come to a halt so they could at least determine whether there was a correlation. They would institute review boards and rigorous standards to oversee future surgeries. Nightly news would investigate and scrutinize medical practices. Politicians would demand congressional hearings.

Several mental health professionals are sounding the alarm about gender transition and its psychological effects. Psychologists Dr. Michael Bailey and Dr. Ray Blanchard claim, "[T]he best scientific evidence suggests that gender transition is not necessary to prevent suicide. . . . There is no persuasive evidence that gender transition reduces gender dysphoric children's likelihood of killing themselves."[56] Child and adolescent psychiatrist Sven Roman states, "There is currently no scientific support for gender-corrective treatment to reduce the risk of suicide."[57] Psychologist Dr. James Cantor discovered that the American Academy of Pediatrics (AAP) misrepresented data to justify its claim that medical transition prevented suicide. The American College of Pediatrics (formed in response to the direction of the AAP) notes the risk of suicide among trans-identified youth is even lower than other at-risk adolescents and that effective suicide prevention for gender-dysphoric adolescents employs the same methods (talk therapy and psychiatric medications).[58]

The professionals who disagree with affective therapy include therapists, sexologists, and psychologists who have earned considerable respect in their fields. They don't consider the question of gender from a biblical worldview. They're not social conservatives. They don't even agree on whether or when children should medically transition. But they do share one professional opinion: they believe gender dysphoria is a psychopathology, "a mental disorder to treat, not primarily an identity to celebrate." Some even say the epidemic among teenage girls isn't gender dysphoria at all, making affirmative therapy either "a terrible dereliction of duty or a political agenda disguised as help."[59]

Thankfully, the tide is beginning to turn. In 2022, U.K.'s National Health Service closed its only gender-identifying clinic for children after a series of scandals.[60] The Tavistock Portman NHS Foundation in London was accused of allowing gender to overshadow other mental issues rather than meet patients' "holistic needs."[61] A leaked 2016 study found that, even after puberty suppression medication, "rates of self-harm and suicidality did not decrease."[62] The results were so scandalous, one of the clinic's governors resigned, stating he feared the clinic was rushing youths into gender transition that didn't help and, in some cases, caused further harm: "The overwhelming feeling was that some children in its care were not being given enough time in their psychological assessment and treatment."[63]

Proponents of gender transition will claim the data reflects a society that is still unaccepting, nonaffirming, and exclusionary. If transgender persons received greater support from their relationships and their environment, we could prevent such a crisis of mental health. Yet society has never been more accepting of gender-nonconforming people. The medical community, mental health professionals, the education system, pop culture and media, and even corporate marketing increasingly prioritize the trans community and focus on their inclusion. If society has become more affirming, why do so many still suffer from the same mental health problems they had before their gender transition?

A study published at 4th Wave Now concluded that when other mental health factors are weighed, the suicide attempt rate among gender-dysphoric people is typically halved, around 20 percent. That's still alarmingly high. But it might demonstrate that gender dysphoria does not require different treatments from other mental health problems. According to Zucker, mental health outcomes for adolescents with and without gender dysphoria are similar. In other words, we can't know or conclude that the teen's suicidal ideation or self-harm tendencies are because of their gender dysphoria or because of the "many other mental health problems that gender dysphoria adolescents so often bear."[64] The condition may correlate with increased suicidality but not necessarily cause it.

Moreover, some psychologists warn the language and frequency of speaking about suicide can create a social contagion. Suicidality can become a "symptom pool" along with feelings of gender dysphoria. The more it occurs and the more people talk about it, the more likely vulnerable girls will harm themselves. Marchiano explains: "When you tell a group of highly suggestible adolescent females that if they don't get a certain thing, they are going to feel suicidal, that's suggestion, and then you're actually spreading suicide contagion."[65] When teen girls are told being denied something will make them suicidal, they become suicidal. It becomes a self-fulfilling idea. Don't hear me wrong—this doesn't imply we should ignore the issue or brush it under the rug. But telling adolescent girls with gender confusion that they are prone to suicidal ideation may only exacerbate the problem.

An organization collaborating with several suicide prevention nonprofits cautions against careless conversations about self-harm. They note that its frequency and prominence can promote the risk of suicide as a social contagion, essentially spreading the vulnerability among already vulnerable people. Admonishments include not referring to suicide as an "epidemic," not referring to it as a common response to hardship, and avoiding speculation as to the reason for suicide.[66] Some doctors condemn the frequent talk of suicide as passive-aggressive manipulation or bullying parents to consent to gender transition. An epidemiologist, himself a former transgender male, calls it a "shameful social engineering strategy," in which activists and clinicians "effectively threaten suicide on behalf of the young people."[67]

The impulse to protect this vulnerable segment of our population is right and good. But it's being misdirected, if not manipulated, by a vocal group of gender activists who seem intent on pushing young patients to embrace trans-identity to the exclusion of addressing other psychological needs. If a teenage girl is in a mental health crisis, the last thing she should do is make irrevocable, life-altering medical decisions. She needs more protection, more intervention, more research to consider, more information, and more input from those devoted to her well-being, not less. Transgender and gender-nonconforming people represent a vulnerable group of our society. They deserve better.

## Conclusion

Affirmative care may temporarily alleviate a person's emotional distress. But it does little, if anything, to resolve the underlying psychological problems that plague young, gender dysphoric girls.[68] Instead, it socially forms a person's sexual and gender identity, shaping the self-perception of vulnerable females. Even more, it drives confused and impressionable young women and girls to avoid addressing their emotional trauma or mental stressors and to locate all their distress in gender identity.

Why have such beliefs and practices taken root in our social consciousness so rapidly? To answer that, the next chapter will consider how philosophical ideas form female identity and affect young women and girls in our gender-confused age.

# CHAPTER 2

# Why: The Ideas That Dominate Our Sense of Self

Take a look at the cleaning products you have around your house. No really, go ahead.

What ingredients do you see? Maybe some ammonia in the window spray, bleach in the bathtub scrub, hydrogen peroxide in the counter spray. Perhaps a little vinegar or rubbing alcohol if you're more into natural cleaning methods. You probably don't think much about your household cleaners. They're pretty common. But mix them with each other, and it's a combination you can't afford to ignore. On their own, they're so common you wouldn't think to notice them. Together they're toxic.

The ideas discussed in this chapter are similar to the cleaning products in your house: they seem common, so familiar you hardly notice them. But mix them together, and they create a toxic combination. Our culture's confusion over female identity is due, in part, to the influence of certain ideas. These ideas, or *philosophies* if we're going to go with the formal term, have shaped us. We have breathed in their contaminated fumes and been formed by the worldviews they espouse. Like most airborne toxins, we're often unaware of their presence until we see their effects.

Throughout this chapter, I reference the research and expertise of Christian philosopher and historian Carl Trueman. I've attempted to distill portions of his 2022 book, *Strange New World*, which itself is a distillation of his larger, 2020 book, *The Rise and Triumph of the Modern Self*.[1] I hope you'll read his works in depth (after you're done with this one, of course).

To navigate our gender-confused culture accurately and effectively, we must first know our surroundings. As you consider these philosophers and how their ideas have formed society's view of gender, keep this in mind: most in the LGBTQIA+ community have little knowledge of the ideas that produced our gender-fluid culture. This chapter isn't about people who struggle with gender identity. It's about the greater ideas that *influence* people who struggle with gender identity (and those who don't, for that matter, as these ideas shape all of us in the modern West).

## Ingredient 1: Post-Christianity—A Kingdom with No King

The first thing we must note about the ideological surroundings in today's American society is that it is post-Christian. The term *post-Christian culture* is becoming more familiar, likely because we can't deny that we're living in one. The phrase has two meanings, and both apply today. First, the Christian faith is no longer a major social influence. Unlike previous generations, those with privileged places of influence or prestige have nothing to do with Christian faith, nor do they typically look on Christian teaching with favor. As a result, Christianity is considered outdated and irrelevant at best, and hateful, bigoted, even dangerous at worst.[2]

Second, in a post-Christian culture, society rejects Christianity's primary claims but hangs on to some of its values. Pastor John Mark Comer describes it as the attempt to move away from the Christian vision for life but still retain its "scaffolding."[3] For instance, Americans still value caring for the poor, pursuing justice for the vulnerable, equality for all, and kindness to strangers. But they largely reject the exclusivity of Jesus as Lord and the authority of the Bible over our lives, particularly concerning sexual ethics. In the words of pastor and author Mark Sayers, a post-Christian culture wants the "solace of faith, whilst gutting it of the costs, commitments, and restraints that the gospel places upon the individual will." It desires the kingdom but without the King.[4]

## Ingredient 2: Postmodernism—"If It Works for You"

The second thing we must note about our American culture's ideological ingredients is that it is postmodern. Postmodernism claims objective truth doesn't exist. Instead, reality is made up of narratives, or social frameworks, created by subjective human beings.[5] Truth, therefore, is not an objective reality we can discover but a subjective experience we create. Social values, moral codes, and religions are the products of human beings. Postmodernists may believe God exists, but they don't believe we can know Him or be certain of His character.[6] Within postmodernism all religions are opinions and products of their culture. No religion is more or less "true" than any other, and to claim otherwise is just a ruse to gain social power. Your Christian faith may "work for you" and be "true for you," but to claim it is universally true for everyone is arrogant and unjust.[7]

Consequently, concepts of right and wrong are relative. Society's moral standards reflect only that particular society, not a high moral law. Certainly not a divine being. What is horrific to one culture may be insignificant to another. What is wrong for me may be right for you.[8] From this we hear phrases like "your truth" or "it's true for you but not for me."

So when a person, system, or worldview makes an objective, absolute claim—such as "God created humanity male or female by design"—a line has been crossed. A statement like that doesn't reflect your feelings, your perspective, or your culture. It reflects a *universal* moral principle with *universal* moral implications about human beings and how they should live. It imposes a moral system onto someone else. And, in the postmodern worldview—where absolute right and wrong don't exist—this is the unforgivable sin.[9]

## Ingredient 3: Expressive Individualism—"Live Your Truth"

If you grew up watching Disney movies, you've absorbed the third thing that is baked into our cultural surroundings: expressive individualism. In fact, you were drinking it down long before you could pronounce it. Expressive individualism says that the inner you is the *real* you, the *authentic* you. This "real you" holds the key to all your happiness and fulfillment.[10] Individual freedom, self-definition, and self-expression are your highest good, and you should pursue them at any cost.[11] Authenticity is your greatest virtue. And inauthenticity, your greatest sin.

Expressive individualism looks to one's feelings to shape and guide one's actions.[12] The deep-seated, psychological core of your identity—your inclinations, your intuitions—must reveal itself for you to be authentic.[13] When your outer world aligns with and expresses your inner world, you are being your "true self." One philosopher described our culture as an "age of authenticity" in which we must express our inner, deeper selves, no matter how they defy expectations or traditions. We must "find and live out" our own understanding of humanity and refuse to surrender to conformity imposed on us by society, previous generations, or religious or political authority.[14]

Expressive individualism affects how we view responsibilities when they conflict with our inner desires. It informs how we relate to our society and community.[15] Anything that gets in the way of our self-expression—tradition, religion, wisdom from others, sacrifices we may be called upon to make, societal restrictions for the common good—must be deconstructed or destroyed.[16]

Someone pursuing her "authentic self" is fulfilling her purpose in life: following her heart.[17] Even more, she is pursuing her own truth—which, as expressive individualism claims, is found within one's self. Like postmodernism, the only wrong response to a person's choices or beliefs is to judge them as wrong.[18] But expressive individualism goes further. It claims inner feelings have ultimate authority over identity. The self is the source of truth.

We can draw a straight line between expressive individualism and modern gender theories. As Carl Trueman observes, just decades ago a psychologist whose patient said he was a woman trapped in a man's body would work to bring the man's mind in line with his body, aligning the man's inner thinking with outer, observable reality. Now, however, a psychologist works to bring the man's body in line with his mind, essentially disagreeing with reality, or rather trying to bend reality toward one person's inner thoughts.[19] What changed? The weight we give inner feelings and one's sense of self. "Psychology trumps biology," Trueman explains. "The language is that of inner feelings, individual experience, and personal sense. The person's own feelings are given such authority that it is hard to see how any person might challenge an individual's view of their own identity without being immediately liable to accusations of oppression or worse."[20]

Expressive individualism explains nearly all the prevailing psychological and medical treatments for gender dysphoria. We see it in affirmative therapy, preferred pronouns, puberty blockers, cross-sex hormones, and surgical procedures. We hear it when pediatricians insist four-year-olds have a stable sense of gender identity. We witness it in elementary school curricula and public policies.

They all boil down to the same idea: the deeper "you" must be uncovered and expressed. And all external hindrances must be removed, even if that means irreversibly mutilating your own body or completely tearing apart the stabilizing fabric that holds together all the major institutional spheres of society.

## Ingredient 4: Distrust of Society—Escape All Social Expectations

There's a funny moment in the TV sitcom, *The Office*, when Michael Scott observes there is something wrong with society. Ever the straight man, Jim Halpert replies, "You're always saying there's something wrong with society, but . . . maybe there's something wrong with you." To which Michael retorts, "If it's me, then society made me that way."

And now you understand philosophical Romanticism. Well, not really, but perhaps a sliver of it.

While expressive individualism may sound modern, its roots go back centuries, stemming from the French philosopher, Jean-Jacque Rousseau. Rousseau is considered the father of Romanticism, a philosophy that continues to be an undercurrent in the West. Rousseau believed our feelings comprised the core of our true selves. He said his life's goal was to "make known my inner self, exactly as it was in every circumstance of my life," a discovery he could make only by looking within himself to access his inner thoughts.[21]

Rousseau held that people were naturally free, independent, and good. But society reshapes them into a hypocritical way of living. Its traditions and obligations hinder them from living according to their inner nature. It condemns them to an inauthentic life. It is the true source of human corruption. If we could tap just into our natural selves, untainted and unswayed by society's demands, we could express our true, authentic natures.[22] In fact, anyone and everyone who tries to change you is an adversary to your true, authentic nature. Relationships and social structures (family, religion, government, etc.) are only valid to the degree they support the real you.[23]

Like most worldviews, it has a grain of truth: we're all affected by our broader culture and moral environment. But Rousseau misdiagnosed the problem of the human condition as well as its source. Indeed, if every single individual within a collective society were pure and good, the whole society would be pure and good. But one quick glance at reality proves otherwise. We are not naturally good (1 John 1:8). Our hearts will not save us from a corrupt society. In fact, our hearts produce the very actions that contribute to a corrupt society (Matt. 15:17–19; James 4:1–3). Society may influence us, yes, but it is made of individuals who have moral agency and personal responsibility for their choices.

You can recognize Rousseau's ideas in the way we express our identity today, especially related to gender. If we can't trust *any* influence apart from our inner selves, then what makes our physical bodies any more trustworthy than other sources of identity? Both society and our own bodies are external to our "true" selves.

Consequently, in this worldview, the more social expectations someone's identity defies, the more courageous she is. Someone who comes out as trans is celebrated and esteemed for being honest and true. Trueman elaborates: "All of this derives from authorizing—indeed, valorizing—that inner voice of nature and then expecting or even demanding that the outside world, from the public square to the individual's body, conform to this."[24] People who throw off social constraints to express their authentic selves are held up as role models.

But this creates a curious dynamic. If society is the source of human corruption, then the best thing society can do is get out of the individual's way and support her self-expression. Social structures that once existed for the *communal* good must adapt their sole purpose to elevate the liberated individual. If they can't or won't, they need to die.

## Ingredient 5: Suspicion of Structures—"It's All About Power"

When Friedrich Nietzsche shocked the world by declaring, "God is dead," he proposed a new way to think about morality: don't. Don't think about it at all. It doesn't exist.

Nietzsche claimed morality was a manipulative tool for social control and religion was for weak-willed simpletons who couldn't think for themselves.[25] His beliefs about morality and religion hinged on his atheism. And what followed was perfectly logical: if God doesn't exist, then moral constraints don't exist. "Shoulds" and "should nots" don't exist. Moral authority is a myth. Obligation to standards is a myth. The expectation that human beings obey a moral code is a myth. Summarizing Nietzsche's moral philosophy, Trueman states, "If there is no God, then we are our own masters. . . . We are to be whatever we want or choose to be. Whatever makes us feel good about ourselves, that is what we should do."[26] Therefore, people should get rid of every moral hindrance that controls them, and they'll be free to live as they want to live and be who they want to be.[27]

The idea that religion is a tool of exploitation stems from the philosophy of Karl Marx. (If you're wondering what in the world Marx has to do with gender ideologies, hang with me. It all connects.) Marx was a materialist, meaning he denied the existence of God and, consequently, any objective moral standard. For Marx, the entire world boiled down to political conflict, and at the core of this conflict was economic control.[28] The social class that controlled the economy (the bourgeoisie) exploited the class that actually did all the work (the proletariat). But the exploited working class couldn't see their own plight. They were blinded by a psychological comfort that soothed their inner pain: religion.

For Marx, religion didn't come from a divine source or authority, but it did give hope to the oppressed with empty promises that made economic injustice more endurable.[29] The ruling class benefitted from religion. It was useful. It protected their economic ambition and solidified their control.[30] Thus, Marx infamously labeled religion the "opium of the people." Religious identity drugged them into perpetuating their own bondage. Religion had to be demolished and debunked so the working class would recognize their oppressed condition and change their social institutions. Get rid of religion, and people would wake up and rise up.

But that wasn't all.

The family was next. Friedrich Engels, collaborator with Marx and coauthor of *The Communist Manifesto*, believed the nuclear family enabled the ruling capitalist class to retain their power. Family relationships meant passing on wealth to one's children. Marriage and family were considered property relationships. Wives and children were capitalist slaves.[31]

Both Marx and Engels believed the communist revolution would diminish differences between men and women.[32] Women who participated in the workforce would have economic freedom and would no longer need to marry for financial security. Economic freedom meant sexual freedom. Liberated from marriage, women could participate in "more unrestrained sexual intercourse" due to a "laxer public opinion regarding virginal honour [sic] and female shame."[33] The key to sexual freedom and social equality required abolishing the family.

These ideas didn't die with nineteenth-century German philosophers. In fact, they've expanded in application. Now a liberated society must not only abolish the family but the categories of man and woman. If social categories of gender serve to protect social institutions like the family, then society should destroy them altogether. We saw this when the 2019 National Socialism Conference, which featured the tagline "No Borders, No Bosses, No Binaries." One of the speakers described pregnancy as a "tool of oppression" and called for Americans to "abolish the family" by "getting rid of capitalism" and restructuring society around the connection between "gender justice" and "economic and social justice."[34] The structure of the family must be dismantled to make way for the individual, particularly the individual's sexual orientation and gender identity.[35]

This is why so many gender activists—those attempting to transform society's institutions by dismantling the family and sexual mores—acknowledge their affinity for Marx's ideas.[36] The honest ones, at least.

## Ingredient 6: Identity and Intersectionality—How We Identify Ourselves

The sexual revolution of the 1960s removed the stigma of sexual license, a social shift enabled by the advent of the birth control pill. Initially it appeared to inaugurate unprecedented equality for women. But decades later its drawbacks were obvious: abortion, increased pornography, widespread divorce, and fatherlessness, a factor even secular sociologists identify as predictive of a child's future stability and success. By detaching sex from pregnancy, sex was also detached from relationships.[37] This introduced a shift in family structures and created a void.

In her book *Primal Screams*, Mary Eberstadt directly correlates the sexual revolution to our culture of identity politics. Eberstadt claims a lack of family identity drove people toward a political identity.[38] The emotions associated with political affiliations or causes, often expressed in visceral and unhinged ways, stem from a culture whose population has been separated from family communities. People are trying to answer questions of identity in political terms. Politics takes the stabilizing place of family.

And, in an already secular society, political activism takes the place of religion. It instills a sense of purpose, identity, higher calling, and even structure.[39] People discover something outside themselves to which they can attach. "In much of what passes for politics these days, we are not seeing reasoned debate," Ederstadt explains, "we are seeing pre-rational assertions of identity."[40] Politics is being driven more by "primordial needs and desires that have been detoured into politics." The identity politics that dominate our social climate explain why rational arguments are so often met with irrational dissent. Opposing views do not merely challenge what someone believes; they challenge who someone *is*.

Intersectionality (how one's minority statuses intersect) and identity politics are linked. Intersectionality began as a legal theory in the early 1990s. Since then it has evolved and permeated how we understand society and the people in it. It also claims to diagnose what's wrong with society along with how to cure it. There are two aspects to intersectionality—descriptive and prescriptive—and we do well to keep them distinct. The *descriptive* aspect refers to how people who represent several social minorities relate to the broader majority culture. These minorities include gender, sexuality, ethnicity, nationality, religion, physical ability, and mental health. The more minorities a person represents, the more her identity "intersects" and the less social power she has.

The *prescriptive* aspect claims one's intersectional identity predicts the degree of oppression and discrimination she has experienced. The greater her intersectional identity—i.e., the more minority statuses she possesses—the more qualified she is to critique society. Her perspective is more reliable, pure, and worthy of following than the perspective of someone who has not had her experiences. And if the core problem of the human condition is the imbalance of power, how do we fix what's wrong with society? We shift the balance of power, elevating the perspectives of those who represent one or more social minorities and minimizing or "decentering" the perspectives of those who have enjoyed privileged majority status. This, intersectionality claims, will create a truly just and righteous society.

Not everything about intersectionality is wrong—a disabled, impoverished immigrant is equally created in God's image and worthy of dignity and respect, but he doesn't have the same advantages and is, therefore, more easily overlooked and exploited. The Lord reserves some of His strongest rebukes to those among His people who exploit the socially vulnerable. But this reflects the descriptive aspect. The *prescriptive* aspect claims that we determine what is true, not according to an objective standard, but according to subjective viewpoints.

This cultural "ingredient" is so common we hardly notice it. We can unknowingly measure whether a viewpoint has value by the social or demographic categories of the person expressing it. This is especially true of gender ideologies. Since transgender identity decenters the privilege of cisgender, heterosexual people, society deems it worthy elevation over and against the socially powerful majority. This is part of why teenage girls who come out as trans receive so much positive attention. They are dismantling "cisheteronormativity."[41]

Gender identity is among the many expressions of identity politics and categories of intersectionality. But unlike other identities, it occupies a privileged place in society. This is because sexual orientation and gender identity (SOGI) is the one aspect of our lives in which all the above ideas collide.

## Ingredient 7: SOGI = Self (Your Sexual Identity Is Your True Identity)

(Note: this section contains references to childhood sexual abuse and rape.)

The sexual revolution didn't just change what was considered acceptable; it rejected the idea of "acceptable" altogether. It removed the stigma of what used to be shameful.[42] Since universal moral codes are an invention of society to keep people under control, human sexuality has no innate moral significance. Consent is the only factor that matters in sexual relationships.[43] All other obligations or hindrances are oppressive and unhealthy.

The roots of this radical shift find their beginning in the theories of psychoanalyst Sigmund Freud. Freud claimed human beings were fundamentally sexual. Sexual drive is the primary force behind all human behavior, sexual desires define human beings,[44] and sexual pleasure is central to human fulfillment.[45] Before Freud sex was an activity for either procreation or recreation; after Freud sex was our identity. It defines who we are as individuals, as societies, and as a species.[46] To deny the impulses of your sex drive is sexual repression and the root of neuroses like chronic stress, anxiety, or depression. Following your sexual impulses, according to this line of thinking, brings health and happiness. Society's moral codes may have been useful to maintain a well-ordered, civilized world, but they didn't reflect standards of right and wrong.[47] Sexual liberation, therefore, became a "moral crusade."[48]

Much of Freud's research has been debunked. But that hasn't eliminated his influence. Researchers like Alfred Kinsey took Freud's ideas even further. Kinsey was a zoologist, which is fitting since he believed human beings were little more than animals. He normalized the belief that sex was just a biological urge, claiming it was "acceptable in whatever form it is manifested."[49] Including with children.

It sickens me to write this. This is the Kinsey that Hollywood doesn't want you to know about.[50]

Kinsey's book, *Sexual Behavior in the Human Male*, claimed sex acts with young children didn't constitute rape. They were merely "sex play." Despite their age, children could "consent" to sexual activity; despite crying and reacting violently, young boys enjoyed being molested; despite hundreds of women describing childhood sexual trauma, there was no lasting damage.[51] In 1949, Kinsey testified before California legislators that the state should lessen penalties for suspected child molesters and that society's "hysteria" over sexual abuse harms children more than the sexual abuse itself.

Today, Kinsey's "research" is used to normalize the sexualization of young children. We can identify a direct correlation between his influence and trends celebrated as "inclusive education." Our society has embraced the belief that sexual liberation is humanity's greatest good, and sexual restraint is humanity's greatest oppression. When an individual's identity is defined by his or her sexual desires, then expressing those sexual desires becomes essential to living an authentic life.[52] Sexual rules validate or invalidate sexual identities. And, when one's sexual orientation and gender identity (SOGI) equals one's entire self, forbidding a type of sexual expression means forbidding a type of person.[53]

This brings us to the last cultural "ingredient": the politicization of sex.

## Ingredient 8: The Politicization of Sex—"Trans Rights Are Human Rights"

If your sexual identity is your "true self" and your "true self" must be expressed, then how society responds to your sexual desires becomes a political question.[54] A law that forbids a certain kind of sexual activity or the manifestation of a certain kind of sexual desire is a law that forbids a certain kind of *person*. Once sex becomes *identity*, sex must also become politicized because identities and their social inclusion are inevitably political.

Psychoanalyst Wilhelm Reich combined the social theories of Marx and the sexual theories of Freud.[55] He was Freud's student and believed sexual satisfaction was the key to social liberation and even medical health. He was known for creating the "orgone box," which Reich believed harnessed the power of sexual energy to cure cancer. (Sean Connery was apparently a big fan during his 007 days.) One media outlet called him a "sexual evangelist," celebrating how he "created a morality out of pleasure."[56] For Reich and his followers, promiscuity became a type of political activism against sexually repressive traditions. Tolerating a person's sexual identity was not enough; society had to affirm one's sexual identity and regard it as equally valid to others. He called this "recognition."[57]

Like Engels, Reich believed dismantling the family was essential for political liberation.[58] "Sexual codes were part of the ideology of the ruling class and designed to keep the status quo, and preserve their power."[59] But Reich took Engels's theories a step further when he fused them with Freud's theories on repressed sexuality.[60] Where Engels focused on the economic liberation of wives, Reich focused on the sexual liberation of children.

Reich believed moral codes aimed to produce compliant children who obeyed their authority figures in patriarchal cultures.[61] The solution to oppressive family structures was an education program that would encourage a child's sexual exploration and expression and would remove hindrances to his sexual gratification.[62] Abolish sexual codes and children will be free individuals, at liberty to express themselves however they desire.[63]

But an obstacle remained. The family, with its insistence on sexual ethics, was "the single most important unit of ideological control for an oppressive and totalitarian regime." Intervention must come from the state. "In short," Trueman explains, "the state has the right to intervene in family matters because the family is potentially the primary opponent of political liberation through its cultivation and policing of traditional sexual codes."[64] To protect the child's sexual and political freedom, the government must be willing to coerce and even punish families that dissented from the state's sex education program.

Reich's ideas have found another expression in our current culture: oppression can be primarily, even exclusively, psychological. For Reich, the state needed to protect children from the oppression of parents who attempted to form their child's sexual morality and gender identity.[65] The government becomes the guardian of an individual's sexual identity.

## Combustible Combinations

These ingredients are strong in themselves, and each of them has a significant cultural presence. They are so pervasive, so ubiquitous, that we hardly notice them. Until they interact with one another. When they do, the results are toxic, danger-ous, and corrosive. Here are a few of the fallouts—see if you can add your own.

"SOGI = Self" mixed with expressive individualism pro-duced affirmative therapy. Distrust of society and expressive individualism encourage the sexualization of children through gender education in elementary schools and Drag Queen Story Hour.[66] Post-Christianity and postmodernism mixed with sus-picion of structures produces a society that vilifies a Christian sexual ethic. Concepts like abstinence, chastity, heterosexual marriage, monogamy, and sexual self-control are no longer regarded as unusual. They are considered oppressive, harmful, and a threat to free society.

Expressive individualism mixed with postmodernism creates a division between gender identity and biological sex. Since we cannot arrive at certainty, we cannot know whether a biological female is a woman or a man. We cannot even know how many genders exist. And, since no worldview has the authority to claim absolute truth, no external standard can judge whether one's gender identity is right or wrong. Not society. Not religion. Not even science or observable reality. If everything is a product of culture, then who's to say a person's gender identity should correlate to biology? For some gender activists, even the presence of binary biological sex is a social construct equated with bigotry. Biology has effectively been "canceled."[67] The categories of male and female are just cultural ideas that have no bearing on one's inner sense of self.

## Conclusion

Each of these ideas has made its way into our social consciousness. Together they form our perspectives on ourselves, our relationships, and our world. And each of them promises a significant life, a liberated life. Transgender or not, there is not one person in Western culture—not you, not me, not anybody—who remains unaffected by these dominating philosophies. These ideas and values shape our thinking about who we are. They affect how we view our relationships, our families, our responsibilities, our professions, and our metrics of success. And they also affect how we measure happiness and fulfillment. Essentially, they influence our identity and how we form our sense of self.

And once female identity in particular has been socially formed and philosophically guided by these ideas, it naturally finds its expression in the sphere of relationships. How she relates to others and how others relate to her validate or invalidate her gendered self-perception. But self-asserted identity is incomplete. We instinctively recognize the need for others to acknowledge and affirm who we are. Female identity, as we will explore in the next chapter, hinges on being relationally confirmed.

# CHAPTER 3

# Where: The Relational Sphere and Validation of Gender Identity

Young Bryony wants to give trans women a quintessentially female experience: a period. With a teaspoon of corn flour, a few drops of food coloring, and some egg whites, trans women can create imitation blood and simulate menstruation.[1] She coaches viewers on how to spoon the "period blood" onto a pad in an authentic pattern, explains how to fill and insert a menstrual cup, and even recommends using a cycle tracking app so they can have regular "periods." "Menstruation is something natural that is constantly associated with being a 'woman,'" Bryony states. "[I]t is completely normal for all women to want to experience this sensation." In other words, if someone is free to identify as a woman internally, that person is free to relate as a woman externally.

At over 1.3 million views, the YouTube video demonstrates the lengths to which transgender people will go, not just to appear or feel like the opposite gender but to relate to themselves and to others in kind.

Gender identity is fundamentally relational. It guides how you interact with others. It shapes your relationships and your identity in them. And it requires a degree of acceptance, both in how we relate to others and in how others relate to us. Your clothes, your hairstyle, your name and pronouns—none of these are the *substance* of your gender. But they do *reflect* your gender and appeal to others to relate to you accordingly. Female identity, then, is relationally confirmed.

And, as scientists perfect the possibility of "womb transplants," giving a biological man the hope of pregnancy,[2] at what point might a man "become" a woman? At what point *is* someone a woman? In this chapter, we explore the processes and procedures people endure in the hope of relating to themselves and others according to their preferred gender and whether these measures can truly change one's gender at all.

## Hairstyles, Hormones, and Hysterectomies

Once a gender-dysphoric girl or young woman assumes a trans identity, she often starts the sequence of life-altering choices known as gender transition. The sequence typically goes like this: *social → hormonal → surgical*.

Social transition is usually the first and fastest way adolescents express their gender dysphoria. A teen may adopt a new name, new pronouns, a new hairstyle, and new clothes. If she attends a public school, she may be reintroduced to her classmates as "Ethan" instead of "Emma," an event her parents may not learn until well after she's been socializing as a boy.[3] Girls can easily obtain a "binder" online to flatten their developing breasts and consult one of the many teen magazine articles on how to use it.[4] Social transitioning can occur at any stage in her development. Up to this point, all the actions taken are mostly reversible.[5]

But a pubescent or prepubescent girl who has been socializing as a boy is less likely to reverse course. Once she begins the gender-transition process, she becomes socially conditioned to living as her preferred gender.[6] The entire sphere of her relationships adapts to a different identity. Pediatrician Michelle Critella describes social transitioning as a "self-fulfilling" pattern; it sets children on a course to further transition methods. When we consider the brain's neuroplasticity, social transition as a member of the opposite gender becomes a repeated and reinforcing behavior. The stronger the behavioral patterns, the more her brain will alter and adapt, and the less she will identify with her biological sex.[7]

Social transition itself demonstrates that our gender identity is relationally confirmed. It is, in Dr. Lisa Marchiano's words, "a communal activity, requiring the buy-in of others. It insists on the community's participation in this new identity. It requires that others accede to certain practices."[8] In other words, social expressions of gender determine how we relate to our world, our relationships, and even ourselves. Not long after initiating her social transition, a girl transitioning into a boy will likely progress to hormonal therapy.

Hormonal transition occurs in two forms: puberty blockers and cross-sex hormones. Puberty blockers, or hormone blockers, are administered to children at or before the onset of puberty. (Their medical name is *gonadotropin-releasing hormone*, or *GnRH drugs*.) These medications suppress puberty so that the child does not develop secondary sex characteristics such as breasts, rounded hips, and a menstruation cycle.

Affirmative-care therapists believe puberty blockers alleviate adolescent anxiety associated with their changing bodies. Puberty is treated like a medical malady to avoid rather than a normal, developmental stage to embrace. Girls can halt their changing hormones by simply expressing their apprehension about the physical changes they experience. The awkwardness of wearing a "training bra," the discomfort of menstruation, or the unfamiliar attention from classmates, for example. Girls who feel uncomfortable with, or even ashamed of, their bodies can escape puberty altogether.

Puberty blockers have been billed as harmless and, according to the Endocrine Society, "fully reversible."[9] Pediatricians assure parents that hormone blockers are "generally considered safe" and beneficial for transgender, genderqueer, nonbinary, or gender-questioning children for whom puberty is "confusing."[10] They claim the treatment will delay "unwanted physical changes that don't match someone's gender identity," an important step for some children who need more time to "explore their options before deciding whether or how to transition."[11] One pediatrician and Planned Parenthood doctor described it as a "pause" on pubertal development, one children can "pick back up" with the ease of pausing a Netflix subscription.

But they're neither harmless nor reversible. Children and adolescents ingest puberty blockers before fully knowing the risks and certainly before reaching an age of consent. Yet pediatricians and psychologists make them as easily accessible as a cough suppressant. It isn't uncommon for teens to receive hormone treatments after their first visit to a therapist.[12] When doctors prescribe puberty-blocking medications within one or two visits, adolescents assume a significant life decision, one that may have a lifelong effect on their relationships, physical well-being, and future fertility.[13] One children's hospital explained some of the long-term effects of puberty blockers included lower bone density, delayed growth plate closure, and less development of genital tissue. But that's just the beginning of the reported side effects. Known and possible reactions include high blood pressure, weight gain, breast cancer, liver disease, disfiguring acne, arrested bone growth, higher risk of osteoporosis, brain swelling, permanent vision loss, and prevention of full brain maturation.[14]

Lupron is perhaps the most publicized puberty-blocking drug. Lupron is an injectable treatment that halts the natural production of hormones. Halting puberty in children was never its primary purpose; doctors prescribed it as a hormone blocker "off label."[15] Its earliest uses were to treat advanced or recurring prostate cancer. It also treats "precocious puberty," a condition in which children begin pubertal development at ages like seven or eight.[16] The side effects are extensive and, in some cases, horrific. Adult women prescribed Lupron for endometriosis describe long-term, debilitating consequences.[17] One woman said the physical pain was so intense she preferred the pain of endometriosis to Lupron's side effects. Another young woman who received Lupron as a thirteen-year-old experienced vision loss, a risk she was never informed about. A twentysomething was diagnosed with degenerative disc disease and fibromyalgia. She had a deteriorated jaw and cracked teeth.[18] Following an investigation, Lupron's label was updated to include warnings for risk of thromboembolism (blood clot), loss of bone density, and convulsions. Among adolescents taking puberty blockers, the risk of bone density loss and consequent osteoporosis is only recently receiving the research and attention it deserves.[19] The FDA currently has more than twenty-five thousand adverse event reports for Lupron products, including more than fifteen hundred deaths. Reactions include suicidal thoughts, stroke, muscle atrophy, tumor growth, and debilitating bone and joint pain.[20]

Cross-sex hormones also affect mental health. Puberty blockers have been linked to depression and other emotional disturbances related to suicide. Trans women receive enough testosterone to increase their hormone levels ten to forty times above average. Past research has documented a significant link between high doses of anabolic steroids like testosterone and major mood disorders including mania, major depression, and psychotic symptoms. Oxford University professor Michael Biggs discussed an experimental trial of puberty blockers in the U.K. and found there was "no statistically significant difference" between the group given puberty blockers and the group given only psychological support. He also reported evidence that, after a year on puberty blockers, girls experienced *more* behavioral and emotional problems and had *even greater* dissatisfaction with their bodies.[21]

The lack of information is intentional. Internal emails from the University of Washington revealed children prescribed puberty blockers showed no "genuine statistical improvement" in their mental health. The school, however, claimed their study of gender-affirming care demonstrated depression and suicidality "plummeted" among patients. Prior to the email leak, a university media manager intended to ignore the misrepresentation due to "extremely positive pick up by mainstream media."[22] Dr. Diane Ehrensaft is a clinical psychologist and associate professor of pediatrics at University of California, San Francisco.

She acknowledges that pubescent and prepubescent patients undergoing gender transition treatments are "not developmentally mature enough to comprehend the full magnitude of irreversible sterilization." You might expect her to reaffirm doctors' responsibility to inform their patients or the need to exercise additional caution and care for prescribing them or their collective oath to "do no harm." But no. Instead, she claims doctors should not "overburden" children and parents with too much information.[23]

The bliss of ignorance comes at a high cost. Puberty blockers deprive children of the most influential factor toward curing their gender dysphoria: puberty. What's more, doctors can't definitively say whether puberty suppression and hormone therapies are effective. We have no long-term study that examines a large group to document the benefits or harms to gender-dysphoric children of suppressing puberty and decades of cross-sex hormone use.[24]

Nearly every patient who uses puberty blockers advances to receiving cross-sex hormones around age sixteen. It's practically a foregone conclusion. (Remember, puberty blockers simply stop the child's natural sex hormones from producing, but cross-sex hormones must be administered to produce the appearance of the opposite gender.) One study found 95 percent of adolescents undergoing "pubertal suppression" transitioned to hormonal injections. At this point people see what they want to see. Does the statistic authenticate the patient's stated gender? Does it prove that doctors correctly identified the children who would persist in their trans identities? Or does it demonstrate that suppressing puberty—the very stage that would have helped them harmonize mentally and emotionally with their biological sex—only reinforces their trans identity? Without the development of secondary sex characteristics or social interaction as a member of their biological sex, what if they just became more invested in their trans identities and less likely to reverse course?[25]

The U.K.'s gender identity clinic, Tavistock, reported a desistence rate of only 1.2 percent among trans-identifying children prescribed puberty blockers. Those who support medical transition see that number as proof that gender-dysphoric children continue to identify as the opposite gender. Those who don't support medical transition see it as "part of a treatment pathway that ushers children towards adulthood identifying as a trans person."[26]

The initial surge of testosterone often gives girls temporary relief—they may have greater feelings of confidence, reduced symptoms of depression, and lower fatigue.[27] Girls may interpret these feelings as proof that they are receiving hormones that align with their true gendered self rather than recognize them as by-products of testosterone itself. In other words, testosterone tends to have these effects regardless of one's gender identity. But the short-lived relief it brings does not validate a female's gender dysphoria. In fact, testosterone's effects only last a short while; many transgender females continue hormone therapy indefinitely. But after the high wears off, the root issues like depression or anxiety return. Testosterone is a temporary fix with permanent consequences.

Cross-sex hormones come with a host of potential side effects. Oral estrogen, given to biological males, can cause thrombosis (blood clots), cardiovascular disease, weight gain, elevated blood pressure, decreased glucose tolerance, gallbladder disease, and breast cancer. Testosterone injections, given to biological females, increase their risk of heart disease, risk of sleep apnea, and insulin resistance, and have unknown effects on breast, endometrial, and ovarian tissues.[28] They are also reported to cause vaginal atrophy and intense uterine cramps.[29]

A young woman can start receiving cross-sex hormones within months, if not weeks, after seeing a gender therapist. If she starts them during her junior year of high school, she'll have developed distinctive masculine features by the time she graduates, including increased facial hair, changes in facial structure, a lowered voice, and broader shoulders. These secondary sex characteristics give the appearance of masculinity. However, since only a person's own naturally created testosterone (meaning nonforeign testosterone) can create primary sex characteristics (i.e., ovaries or testicles), cross-sex hormones are limited in their effect.[30] Put differently, if a girl receives cross-sex hormones, the risks to her entire female body are widespread and severe, but the results of manufacturing male characteristics are local and limited. If you're thinking the trade-off isn't worth it, you're right. Cross-sex hormones will not give her the body she ultimately wants, but they will wreck the body she has.

Testosterone shots are alarmingly easy to obtain, especially for young adults navigating the newfound stressors of college life. Obtaining cross-sex hormones is as accessible as a visit to the local Planned Parenthood, one of the largest suppliers of testosterone to biological females.[31] One young woman shared how, at eighteen, a nurse practitioner at Planned Parenthood gave her four times the typical starting dose of testosterone on her first trip. She never even saw a doctor. Universities make cross-sex hormones as accessible as antibiotics. Yale University's health insurance plan offers testosterone injections for $10 per month. At Rutgers University, students don't even need a referral—just "informed consent."[32]

Which leads to the final stage of gender transition: gender-reassignment surgery.

Gender-reassignment surgery, also called "gender-confirmation surgery," involves the amputation of reproductive organs and plastic surgery to construct organs of the opposite sex. Male-to-female surgery includes gonadectomy, penectomy, and the creation of a vagina (vaginoplasty) using the skin of the penis and scrotum. The neurovascular bundle of the penis is refashioned to become a clitoris.[33] Patients also undergo electrolysis and laser treatments to remove facial and body hair. Female-to-male (FtM) surgery includes oophorectomy, vaginectomy, and hysterectomy. Metoidioplasty will "exteriorize" or bring forward the clitoris to create a penis, and a mechanical device is implanted in a cosmetic penis (phalloplasty) to enable erections. The labia is also reconstructed to create prosthetic testicles.[34] Overall, FtM surgeries have more complications.

Not all gender reassignment surgeries are successful. The "neovagina" or "neopenis" is constructed from the patient's existing reproductive organs or, in some cases, skin grafted from the patient's arm. Several trans women (biological males) report that, even after healing from "bottom surgery," their new vagina smells like feces, likely because some vaginoplasty procedures construct the neovagina from the colon, and the skin retains the bacterial flora of that anatomy. Others note the loss of sexual function or incapacity for arousal.[35]

Sadly, for many trans-identifying females, the challenges don't end there. Despite medical advancements in hormone therapies and surgical procedures, they may never find relief from their gender dysphoria. Some patients report the gender surgeries alleviated their dysphoria and gave them greater fulfillment. Others report the surgeries worsened their psychological symptoms. Post surgery, they don't feel like a man *or* a woman. Their gender identity—and consequently, how they relate to others—is still out of sync with their bodies. Doctors can't predict which patients will be healed by gender-transition procedures and which patients will be harmed by them. There is no objective standard to determine those who will feel happy, satisfied, and hopeful post operation and those who will feel depressed, regretful, and hopeless.[36]

Dr. Marcus Evans served as clinical director of Adult and Adolescent Services in the United Kingdom's only state-run gender clinic, the Tavistock and Portman NHS Trust. The Tavistock clinic was the largest pediatric gender clinic in the world. In 2019, Evans resigned over his belief the clinic was rushing adolescents into a medical transition: "I saw children being fast-tracked onto medical solutions for psychological problems, and when kids get on the medical conveyor belt, they don't get off." Because the issue was so politicized, methods were not up to the "clinical rigor" they should have been and vulnerable teenagers received treatments they might later regret.[37] In 2022, the U.K. closed the Tavistock clinic entirely after a review concluded that the Gender Identity Development Service (GIDS) was not a "safe or viable long-term option."[38] Perhaps more countries will follow suit.

## The "Whatness" of "Womanness"

By now you've heard the story and seen the memes. Then Supreme Court nominee, Katanji Brown Jackson, was asked to give a definition for the word *woman*. The question aimed to draw out Judge Jackson's views on gender theory and law, a lightning-rod topic for politicians whose rhetoric typically devolves into sound bites and clichés. Justice Jackson replied, "No. I can't. . . . I'm not a biologist." While Judge Jackson is no doubt a brilliant legal scholar, her hesitance to offer a simple definition to a simple question became the stuff of punch lines.

And among her critics were some unlikely sources: gender activists. For gender scholars, Justice Jackson's answer was a commendable attempt but still missed the mark.[39] For not even a competent biologist could provide a definitive answer to the question. Scientists can't agree on a sufficient way to determine what makes a human being a woman and includes the billions of women past and present: "There isn't one single 'biological' answer to the definition of a woman. There's not even a singular biological answer to the question of 'what is a female,'" claims one gender theorist.[40]

In the thousands of years' worth of recorded history, has all of humanity gotten it wrong until the last couple decades? Has every culture in every place at every time misunderstood something so basic to human nature as whether a person is a woman? Have we really become so enlightened that not even Aristotle's logic can contend with our modern gender theories?

Why is defining *woman* such a controversial question?

In her book, *The Genesis of Gender*, Abigail Favale explores this question. She observes society can't find a definition that applies to all women at all times because it's starting from a flawed foundation: no single trait or characteristic is universal to every woman—what Favale calls "actuality."[41]

Think about it. What *do* all women have in common? Try to define a woman according to a single, shared trait. The typical responses would be something like these: women have a uterus. Women can have babies. Compared to men from the same ethnic heritage, women are generally shorter. Women are more inclined to collaborate. But what about a female born with a reproductive disorder? Is she not a woman? What about a female with lifelong infertility? Or a WNBA player? Or Margaret Thatcher? Are these females disqualified from being women because they lack a characteristic the majority of other females possess? No matter what characteristic you choose, someone falls outside the definition yet is, nonetheless, a woman.

Favale has a solution. Rather than define a woman according to actuality (characteristics or traits every woman has in common), we must begin with *potentiality*. What purpose does every woman have the potential to fulfill in a way that excludes men? For Favale, potentiality defines a woman as "the kind of human being whose body is organized around the potential to gestate new life."[42] Understanding womanhood in terms of potentiality for gestation grounds gender in biology. It is the "whatness" of a woman.[43]

This aspect applies to every female, no matter her age, ethnicity, or status. Even if a woman does not desire to gestate new life or is physically unable to gestate new life because of age or irregularity (actuality), her reproductive system is still arranged according to ability to gestate new life (potentiality). In fact, Favale believes the category of infertility itself affirms this definition.[44] A male human being who cannot get pregnant isn't called "infertile"; his reproductive system was never organized for gestation. For a female, however, infertility "names the often painful and devastating inability to actualize one's procreative potential."[45] Her reproductive system falls short of the inherent potential the female body has. A woman may not bear children for any number of reasons. But every woman's anatomy remains structured for the potential of gestating new life. It's how God designed the female body. And this design informs and indicates her identity as a woman.

Defining a woman according to a shared, inherent characteristic that signifies "womanness" is known as "essentialism." Essentialism is the idea that all women possess an "intrinsic property" that makes them women. For gender theorists, *essentialism* is a bad word. It means that men and women are fundamentally different (not necessarily opposite, but different) and that they both have characteristics the other does not.[46] Gender ideology affirms a "constructivist" view of gender, which claims gender differences are merely created or constructed by society.[47] It's all a "performance," in the words of gender theorist Judith Butler. People are simply following a social and relational script. Gender is something we do, not something we are.[48] The body has no "intrinsic meaning," and we can use technology to "give it whatever meaning we want."[49] If society produced one type of gender performance, it could just as easily produce another one.

Favale notes one more "-ism" of gender theory: nominalism. Nominalism claims reality is just a collection of items we have named. There are no overarching definitions of anything. For instance, "virtue" doesn't really exist; instead humans just group ideas together and relate to them as "virtue." Maleness and femaleness don't really exist; they're just products of language and thought.[50] Nominalism, Favale explains, is "the idea that we can group things together in name only, without appealing to a universal essence that transcends culture. I can say, for example, that women exist, because the idea of woman exists as a mental and social construct."[51]

Herein is the logic justifying terms like "penis-having women" and "pregnant men." Female reproductive anatomy becomes detached from the greater concept of womanhood and, consequently, is a disconnected collection of anatomical parts.[52] The disconnection severs reproductive anatomy from any universal purpose.

The result of all this? Dehumanization. Females are "bleeders and breeders." A "vagina" is a "front hole."[53] Breasts are "top parts." "People with a cervix" can become "chest-feeders." This language is part of our cultural vernacular. In 2020, *Teen Vogue* promoted a "101 guide to masturbation for vagina owners." Tampax celebrated "the diversity of all who bleed." The American Cancer Society recommends Pap smears for "individuals with a cervix."[54] The physical body has nothing to do with relational identity; the word *woman* no longer belongs to female personhood at all.[55]

This view of humanity ascribes little to no value to the human body. No transcendent meaning. No divinely bestowed design. Instead, one's reproductive system and, subsequently, the entire physical self, is just a collection of anatomical parts. The true self is exclusively emotional, totally divided from physical reality. As a result, being a man or a woman becomes disconnected from maleness or femaleness entirely.

## Sentiments and Stereotypes

Yet the search for proof of "womanness" continues. If we disconnect a woman's identity from her reproductive potentiality, we're left to define a woman in psychological and socially transient terms. And absent biological sex, its only evidence is cultural expressions and internal feelings. "Bereft of biological markers to explain who counts as a woman," Shrier observes, "trans activists rely on social stereotypes, many of them archaic or insulting."[56] The popular website, The Gender Dysphoria

Bible, tells the female reader if she wants to be a boy, she already is a boy. "Men want to be men, and women want to be women. If you want to be a man, then you're a man. It really is that simple." Disconnected from the body, the substance of gender is nothing more than a feeling. Another online source recommends those questioning their gender (in this case, MtF) choose small activities to confirm their identity, like shaving their legs, wearing makeup, getting nail polish, or buying female clothing, then observing how they feel. The essence of gender is confirmed in "doing what makes you happy."[57]

Time out.

What about cultures where women don't wear nail polish or women who refuse to shave their legs? You mean to tell me Tyra Banks is less of a woman because she doesn't shave her legs?![58] Expressions of gender differences vary from culture to culture. What one society or time period considered masculine or feminine will be different from another. Just think of the color pink, which used to be considered a masculine color. But historically there are still only two variations. Debra Soh claims whether one gravitates toward or identifies with traits that are masculine or feminine within his or her own culture is based on biology.[59] Moreover, even though social markers for gender change, this doesn't mean children are socialized into having a gender they otherwise wouldn't. While the expression of gender changes depending on what is considered male and female typical, gender is still grounded in biology.[60] Take away the essential biological grounding of womanhood, and it's just a feeling or an activity. The idea that a man can feel like a woman trapped in a man's body "presupposes that someone who has a man's body, a man's brain, a man's sexual capacities, and a man's DNA can know what it is like to be a woman," Anderson explains.[61] "If girlness and boyness no longer reside in the body, there is no other ground for these concepts except stereotypes," Favale states.[62]

Curiously, those within the trans community still ask the same questions about their gender identity. Even after some degree of transition, many wonder whether they are "trans enough." Why don't they feel at home in their trans identity? What if they're still exploring? Why don't they feel as confident in their gender as other trans people? These are the same introspections of those who are gender questioning. At its core, the question asks, "Do I really belong here?" One article attempts to reassure readers that, provided they are being authentic and true to where they are in their journey, they are trans enough: as long as you are exploring, you are the only one who gets to define what your gender means to you. And as long as you're authentic, where you are on your journey is "enough."[63] Again, separate gender from the body, and no one really knows what a woman (or a man) is.[64]

But if female identity *is* essential to being a woman, then even the most advanced surgical skills cannot change a woman into a man. Gender transitions may create "feminized men or masculinized women," but doctors cannot make trans women become actual women, or trans men become actual men.[65] The labia can be constructed into prosthetic testicles, but it cannot produce sperm. A clitoris can be refashioned as a neopenis to achieve an erection, but it cannot inseminate a female. Surgeons can create the *appearance* of a reproductive organ by constructing an artificial anatomy, but without connecting it to reproductive function, they cannot create *actual* reproductive organs. "Plastic surgery on the reproductive organs," Anderson explains, "no matter how 'realistic' the result may appear, does not create the organs of the opposite sex."[66] Only if a penis or vagina can fulfill its biological and reproductive purpose can it properly be called a penis or a vagina, and that would require the recreation of the "entire biological context within which those realities" exist.[67] It's humanly impossible.

Thus, we might say that a biological male perceives himself to be a woman or is uncomfortable being a man. But this doesn't make him a woman. Not when "every cell in his body speaks against it."[68] The idea of gender as separate from biological sex is "incoherent" since it refers either to cultural forms, some of which actually are connected to biology (like how we consider the comfort of pregnant women) or to perceptions and feelings, some of which may not even correspond to reality.[69]

## Conclusion

Step back from the cultural rhetoric of gender identity, and you start to see a pattern. An ironic, self-contradicting pattern. Women are more than their feelings, but if you feel like you're a woman, then you are one. No one can definitively tell you what gender you truly are, but if you even question your identity, the Internet says you're definitely born in the wrong body. The single most influential factor in outgrowing childhood gender dysphoria is experiencing puberty, but if you have childhood gender dysphoria, you're prescribed puberty blockers. Being a woman is *not* clothing designs, color preferences, hairstyles, and other gender expressions, but if you're transitioning from male to female, those exact gender expressions are how you tell the world you *are* a woman. "Gender" is a socially created construct, yet the surge in transgender identity is also a socially created construct. Even a teenager's tutorial on how to fake a period and a doctor's ingenuity for gender-reaffirming procedures reveal how self-refuting gender ideology is: a trans person's anatomy and biological processes are considered completely irrelevant to her gender (i.e., "Gender is *not* about breasts or reproductive organs."), yet when one decides to fully transition, having the anatomy and biological processes of the opposite gender is suddenly considered essential.

For "woman" to be anything more than a stereotype or sentiment, it must be anchored in physical reality. Gender is *distinct* from biology, but it is still *derived* from biology. Apart from biology, female identity is reduced to an impression of one's imagination. Please don't mistake my candor for callousness; gender dysphoria is an unimaginably difficult condition. But it is a condition of the mind, not the body. Female identity is confirmed by how it relates to others. And these relationships are inextricably (although not exclusively) grounded in one's reproductive potential. Thus, we can say, concisely and confidently, that a woman is an adult human female. For even greater proof, we'll consider the physiological and neurobiological differences between male and female in the next chapter.

# CHAPTER 4

# What: The Biological Differences Too Complex to Ignore

You know what a labyrinth is, right? Depending on your age, you may be thinking of that scene in *Harry Potter and the Goblet of Fire*. Or, if you're a child of the eighties like me, David Bowie and some really creepy Muppets. A labyrinth is a complex maze, full of paths and passages. You can get lost in it for hours and still not discover all of it.

Discovering the information for this chapter was like entering a labyrinth, full of wonder and impossible to exhaust. I found myself in awe of the intricate human complexities that start at the cellular level and shape our identities in profound ways. The differences between male and female begin long before families or societies have a chance to form our self-perception. Our biology doesn't just indicate our gender identity; it influences our gender identity.

*How* we think is a lot more complicated than *what* we think.

You're familiar with the phrase, "nature versus nurture." It's a recurring question: What patterns can we attribute to biology (nature), and what can we attribute to society (nurture)? But this perennial debate presents to us a false dilemma, making us believe we have to choose. Instead of an either/or, the relationship between nature and nurture is more of a both/and. Our sex differences begin at the most fundamental human level and influence our behavior from the womb, but human beings are more than machines with highly functioning brains. Our identities run deeper than the expectations we've received from society, but our gendered relationships and interactions shape how our brains function. We are, inescapably, grounded in biology.

The binary differences between male and female biology aren't limited to our reproductive anatomy; they reach every aspect of our biology. This reflects a concept called "sexual dimorphism." Sexual dimorphism means males and females of the same species have genetic differences that produce different attributes and traits. Many of these attributes and traits have nothing to do with reproductive anatomy. Ever notice how male cardinals are more brightly colored than female cardinals? That's sexual dimorphism. Male and female human beings have cellular and molecular differences that affect their entire bodies, including their hearts, lungs, and joints. In the words of one cardiologist: "Every cell has sex."[1]

For at least 99 percent of us, our biological sex is our gender.[2] The phrase "sex assigned at birth" can be appropriate for the 1 percent of people with an intersex condition,[3] but for everyone else, it's a misuse of a term that describes a fraction of developmental sex disorders.[4] In the words of biologist Colin Wright: "In humans, transgender and so-called 'non-binary' people are no exception, this reproductive anatomy is unambiguously male or female over 99.98 percent of the time."[5]

Chromosomes, genes, and hormones work together elaborately connected in a fascinating cause-and-effect system. The developmental differences between male and female affect much more than our reproductive system. Science is still catching up to the psalmist when he said God formed his inmost being in the "secret place." Only God could even think up such a masterpiece.

## Beyond Nature Versus Nurture

Before considering these neurological differences, we must keep three facts in view: first, these patterns represent averages. Averages are not absolutes.[6] For every neurological difference we find between the two sexes, there are exceptions and nearly always overlaps.[7] One neuroscientist explains that everyone's brain has a "mosaic" of female and male traits.[8] The brain-based differences between male and female represent generalities and cumulative averages.[9]

Second, just as our physical bodies are "sexually dimorphic" (males have testes, females have ovaries; males have greater muscle mass than females; etc.), our brains are as well. But in less obvious ways. On the one hand, there aren't "male brains" and "female brains"—the central nervous system of both sexes has the same elements (cerebellum, frontal lobe, brain stem, etc.). But, on the other hand, male and female brains function differently. The brains of both sexes are a "mosaic of malelike and femalelike features."[10] Scientists gauge those differences in terms of comparison and measure them along a continuum. So you'll find phrases like *male brains tend to*, and *female brains often*, etc. to reflect these relative differences.[11]

Third, neurological differences between male and female do not justify stereotypes or discrimination. Clinical psychologist and professor of developmental psychopathology at Cambridge University, Simon Baron-Cohen, explains: "[L]ooking for sex differences is not the same as stereotyping. The search for sex differences enables us to discover how social and biological influences act on the two sexes in different ways, but it does not tell us about individuals. . . . Stereotyping reduces individuals to an average, whereas science recognizes that many people fall outside the average range for their group."[12] Another neuroscientist described the brain-based differences between male and female as "two different types of brains with equally intelligent behavior."[13] We can honor a person's individuality and uniqueness as well as the created, complementary differences between male and female.

## "A Machine Built for Connection"

For the first seven weeks of gestation, male and female embryos develop the same way. But something significant happens at the eighth week, one that will shape brain development in the womb and influence behavior after birth.[14] If the embryo is male, he receives a flood of testosterone. This hormonal surge is so transforming, biologists call it "prenatal puberty." It saturates his system and "masculinizes" his nascent brain by creating structural changes. Certain brain circuits, like those controlling motor and spatial skills as well as sex aggression, start to grow.[15] Others, like those controlling communication and language, are suppressed.[16] This prenatal testosterone will continue to shape the baby's body and brain and will affect his behavior from his first days after birth.[17]

An eight-week-old female embryo does not receive this flood of testosterone. The absence of that hormonal surge also shapes her nascent brain but in an entirely different way. She develops greater connections in the centers that testosterone "killed off" in a male embryo. The lack of testosterone enables the areas that control communication, observation, and the processing of emotion to grow.[18] Preborn girls even behave differently in the womb than male babies.[19] And they enter the world hardwired for communication, connection, and empathy.[20]

Baron-Cohen defines *empathy* as the "drive to identify another person's emotions and thoughts, and to respond to them with an appropriate emotion." Empathy is more than observing someone's emotions. It is tuning into a person's thoughts and feelings, feeling concern for someone, and having a desire to alleviate another's pain or distress.[21] It involves an emotional reaction to the emotions of others to understand them, anticipate their behavior, and connect with them.[22] This doesn't imply that males are incapable of empathy (despite what many women may think) but rather that females, on average, "spontaneously empathize" with others to a greater degree.[23]

The empathy-wired baby girl begins expressing herself within hours after birth. Less than one day old, female newborns are more responsive to the cries of other babies. Within her first few days, she prefers to look at people rather than objects.[24] Infant girls also make sustained eye contact with their caregiver, called "mutual facial gazing." In her first three months, eye contact and mutual facial gazing increase by 400 percent, developing her "innate skill in observation."[25] By contrast, baby boys prefer to look at mechanical objects, especially things in motion.[26]

A female infant is more adept at reading and interpreting facial expressions and hearing emotional vocal tones.[27] As young as one year old, she is more emotionally responsive to the distress of other people, especially if they appear sad or hurt.[28] She starts talking earlier and responds to seeing people's faces more enthusiastically.[29] At eighteen months, she can tell if someone is listening to her by interpreting the person's facial expression and eye contact.[30] As her brain develops, she becomes even more perceptive to people's emotions, has a greater sensitivity to social experiences involving people's faces and emotions, and interprets emotional vocal tones and unspoken cues.[31]

Baby girls also experience what's called "infantile puberty." This is a twenty-four-month period in which an enormous amount of estrogen floods her system and "marinates" her brain.[32] This additional estrogen prompts the development of ovaries and stimulates developing brain circuits in the centers for observation, communication, tending and caring, and even "gut feelings."[33] Apparently a "woman's intuition" has a neurological basis!

We see these differences when children play or make up stories. As young as nine months old, boys and girls will gravitate toward gender-typical toys (i.e., girls to dolls and boys to cars). As Dr. Debra Soh observes, this age is before children are old enough to recognize gender as a concept, which usually occurs between eighteen and twenty-four months. This trait isn't exclusive to human females either: Rhesus and vervet monkeys demonstrate the same patterns, with young females choosing dolls and young males choosing wheeled toys.[34] Both human and primate females showed greater interest in babies, looking at them, cuddling them, even worrying about them.[35] Girls tend to like stories that are warm and nurturing. Boys like stories with conflict, even violence ("good guys and bad guys," "war," etc.). This pattern is so deeply ingrained that if a five-year-old boy makes up a violent (as in, conflict-oriented) story, it's considered normal—he's being a typical boy. But when a five-year-old girl demonstrates a preference for making up violent stories, it often indicates a psychiatric disorder.[36]

Louann Brizendine, a neuropsychiatrist and professor at the University of California in San Diego, describes the female brain as a "machine built for connection."[37] The brain's emotional centers are more active. The *hippocampus*, which is connected to memory and emotion, is also larger in females, meaning they usually have better memories of emotional details.[38] The limbic system, which is linked to bonding, nesting, and one's connection to emotions, is larger and deeper in women.[39] A region of the temporal lobe that's associated with language and verbal fluency, is also larger.[40] And her lower levels of testosterone lead to stronger communication and social skills as well as greater eye contact.[41] Women often have a greater emotional connection to memories[42] and fine-tuned emotional receptivity.[43] Long before "nurture" has an effect on gender identity, "nature" influences female identity and behavior.[44]

This is just the beginning of neurological differences between male and female. Even how they process information differs. Males process information using only the left hemispheres of their brain. Females process information bilaterally, meaning the left and right hemispheres of their brains pass information back and forth. The part of the brain that connects the two hemispheres is called the *corpus callosum*, and it's up to 25 percent larger in females.[45] In 2014, University of

Pennsylvania researchers studied the brain images of 428 young males and 521 young females—a huge sample size compared to other studies. They found that male brain activity was more "tightly coordinated" within specific brain centers, while female brain activity coordinated more strongly between the two hemispheres.[46] Essentially, the two hemispheres of the female brain talk to each other more often.

How our brains process information produces greater average strengths. Another study found male brains have 6.5 times more "gray matter." Gray matter makes up the brain's information processing centers. Female brains, however, have nearly ten times more "white matter." White matter connects or networks those processing centers.[47] Males are usually better at focusing on fewer topics with greater intensity. They can communicate about a specific topic in-depth, but they are less adept at connecting it to other topics or emotions.[48] There was one exception to the white/gray matter difference: language.[49] In just the part of the brain responsible for verbal fluency and verbal memory tasks, females have 20 percent more *gray* matter than males.[50]

One of the scientists behind this study said this may explain why men often excel at activities that require "local processing" of information (like math) and women often excel at activities that integrate and assimilate that information.[51] (Incidentally, a former Google exec was condemned and fired when he claimed biological differences accounted for the company's gender gap.[52])

Remember these studies show generalities and averages, not competence or intelligence. Women are just as capable of excelling in STEM fields, lest we forget the scientist who figured out how to send a man to the moon was a woman.[53] And men are just as capable of expressing emotion; some of history's greatest poets are men. But these averages still demonstrate patterns that are distinct between male and female. The hormonal and neurological differences between boys and girls begin *in utero*, continue into childhood and adolescence, and produce what we would call gender-typical behavior. In Cahill's words, we "come out of the womb" with built-in cognitive biological differences.[54]

## Conversational Differences

All this affects how a female communicates with others. The average female excels in verbal abilities, as well as reading comprehension and writing ability.[55] Female communication comes with greater emotional comprehension, in part because emotions are processed on the right side of the brain.[56] Since men process information on the left side of the brain, their communication tends to be less emotional and less distracted by contextual cues.[57] This is also why women tend to be better at multitasking and maintaining multiple considerations at once.[58]

As girls mature and approach puberty, they are even more inclined toward emotional connections and communication. They develop greater sensitivity to social experiences that involve faces and emotions and process facial expressions more quickly.[59] They find emotional fulfillment in one-on-one friendships and are more expressively affectionate.[60]

The differences between male and female friendships are magnified in the teen years. Whereas a teenage boy needs to be respected and higher in the male hierarchy, teenage girls need to feel socially connected and liked.[61] The typical teen girl, "nontestoteronized, estrogen-ruled" is highly invested in preserving harmonious relationships.[62] On a molecular and a neurological level, she is motivated to ease and even prevent social conflict.[63] The neurological urge to stay connected and make social bonds based on communication means she typically prefers to avoid conflict in her relationships.[64]

Relational conflict and social rejection are highly stressful events for the female brain. They create a "cascade of negative chemical reactions."[65] When a girl's relationships are threatened or lost, she experiences a steep drop in serotonin, dopamine, and oxytocin, and the body's stress hormone—cortisol—takes over.[66] Girls are wired to keep social harmony, and disruptions to that harmony can be deeply distressing, even traumatic.[67] (To the reader having flashbacks to mean-girl-middle-school drama . . . you and me both!) The effects of conflict and rejection for teen girls can be devastating.

Whereas boy friendships are more "shoulder-to-shoulder" around a shared activity or interest, girl friendships are more "face-to-face,"[68] spending time communicating and nurturing their relationship. Rank and hierarchy organize the camaraderie among boys but destroy the friendships among girls.[69] For little boys, competition is about an ability, whereas for little girls, competition tends to be more relational. Just think of how often little girls talk about who is whose "best friend."[70] And she'll cultivate these emotional connections through talking.

A lot of talking. Conversation is central to friendships between women. Language is the glue that cements female bonds.[71] Combine higher language fluency with their drive for connection, and women use language differently from men. For females, language is the tool they use to develop and maintain "intimate reciprocal relationships."[72] Females find *biological* comfort in verbal communication, especially when their communication involves self-disclosure.[73] Sharing secrets or revealing fears activates the pleasure and reward centers of the female brain. When girls connect through talking, their brains get a huge

hormonal rush of dopamine and oxytocin that creates emotional bonds and reduces stress.[74] When girls experience stress,
they look for support from their friends.[75] So, your typical teen
girl who is glued to her smartphone and constantly texting her
friends may be trying to alleviate her adolescent angst through
communication.

Women tend to have a stronger emotional connection to
their personal memories. They retain emotional events more
strongly and vividly than do men. They also recall them more
quickly and with greater intensity[76] and are better able to retrieve
information from their long-term memories.[77]

Women are also twice as likely as men to experience clinical depression and post-traumatic stress disorder.[78] Between the
ages of fourteen and twenty-five, depression is twice as prevalent
among women than men.[79] Female hormone fluctuations tend to
make them more vulnerable to depressive symptoms. Males typically synthesize estrogen faster than females, which makes them
comparatively less vulnerable to depressive symptoms.[80] While
depression may not be exclusively caused by biology, it is influenced by biology. Women are also more likely to have anxiety-
related disorders and internalize their emotions, often resulting
in withdrawal and loneliness. Men, however, are more likely to
externalize their emotions, which often results in aggressive,
impulsive, and noncompliant behavior.[81]

Chronic diseases occur at different rates between males
and females. Estrogen is linked to lower occurrences, or delayed
onset of, certain brain diseases, like Alzheimer's.[82] The hormone has been described as a neuroprotective "shield" against
cognitive decline in aging.[83] Men are more vulnerable to major,
life-threatening diseases like cancer, cirrhosis of the liver, kid-
ney disease, and emphysema. Women are more vulnerable to

suffering from disorders like thyroid and gallbladder conditions, migraine headaches, arthritis, and eczema.[84] Females respond differently to medicines than males.[85] They even manifest different heart attack symptoms.[86]

There are thousands of nonreproductive differences between males and females, many of which influence gender-typical behaviors. For instance, women are biologically wired to cry more frequently than men. Because female tear ducts are smaller, women's tears can spill out more quickly.[87] Females have more sensitive hearing than males, typically hearing sounds eight decibels louder. Little girls may be more likely to feel shouted at not only because of their increased sensitivity to vocal tones but because they hear people's voices more loudly.[88]

Other sex-based physical differences include average height (females are about 9 percent shorter), bone mass and density (females have 50 percent less), and facial structure (females have a rounder jawline and a more pointed chin). The female torso is longer, which accommodates her additional reproductive organs and gives space for the organs to move during pregnancy. The female pelvis is not only wider and longer but also held together by ligaments that soften to accommodate pregnancy.[89]

Finally, body composition differs between males and females.[90] Females are comprised of 30 to 35 percent muscle compared to males' 40 to 50 percent. The only way a female could build comparable bulk or strength to a male is to artificially raise her androgens to a dangerous level.[91] Women typically have 40 percent less upper-body strength, and 33 percent less lower-body strength.[92] Women also have 18 to 20 percent body fat compared to men's 10 to 15 percent. This higher fat-to-muscle ratio allows women to sustain and nourish an unborn baby; the female body stocks up its own fat reserves in anticipation of future pregnancies.[93]

Women's muscles contain 27 to 35 percent more "slow-twitch" fibers than men's muscles as well as a greater density of capillaries.[94] This combination enables women to sustain force for an extended period of time but not generate a significant burst of force. Basically, her muscles probably can't pull a car by a rope, but they can endure sustained contractions without quitting.[95] Down to the muscle fibers, the female body is structured and organized around sustaining new life.

I know. Pretty amazing, right?

These biological differences represent one of the many factors that influence the development of sex identity. Psychologist Richard Lippa identifies several elements including family and peer influences, how someone thinks about gender-related emotions and attitudes, and even someone's behavior. He calls these influences "causal cascades" because of the way they spill into and affect the other.[96] Biology isn't the only factor in our identity. But it is an important one. If we ignore the reality of biology or dismiss it as a "social construct," we'll miss how sex-specific differences are influencing a generation of gender-confused females.

Relational connectedness. Retention of negative emotions. Bonding through conversation. What if the surge of trans-identifying adolescent and young women is partly due to girls being . . . girls? What if the inherent femaleness of vulnerable young women, and all the tendencies that come with it, is being exploited by gender ideology on a mass scale? The neurobiological makeup of female identity alone would seem to make women and girls more susceptible to beliefs and ideas that manipulate their nature.

## Conclusion

The biological differences between male and female are not just different but different in corresponding ways—what J. Budziszewski calls "polaric complementarity." Male and female are "complementary opposites—alike in their humanity, but different in ways that make them natural partners. Each sex completes what the other lacks, and helps bring the other into balance."[97] This brings us to the last question of female identity: Who is she?

Is there a meaning to female identity as a sexed body and a gendered self? And, consequently, does sexual differentiation between male and female have significance beyond reproduction?

If the answer is no, then the sexed body has no intrinsic meaning, purpose, or value. But if it's yes, then female identity would have to involve a bigger idea, a goal, a *telos*. Viewing human nature through the lens of its *telos* provides a foundation to affirm its transcendent dignity: "Sexual dimorphism is not a negative limitation imposed by nature," Nancy Pearcey explains. "Nor is it an oppressive move by the dominant culture. It is a positive, healthy form of interdependence that speaks of our creation as social beings designed for loving, mutual interdependence in marriage, families, and communities."[98] The sex-based differences between male and female are imprinted on our physical bodies. They reflect God's design that human beings are not independent of but interdependent on each other. Cultures change. Value systems evolve. But this reality transcends what is temporal and points to human purpose. As we'll explore next, the ultimate purpose of female identity is theological.

## CHAPTER 5

# Who: The Theological
# Meaning of Female Identity

It feels like a lifetime ago, but I used to play the harp.
I remember discovering how plucking certain strings
together created harmony. Octaves produced a sense of
emphasis, and that makes sense; it's the same note in different
degrees. But harmony produces beauty—the tightness of thirds,
the depth of sixths, the richness of tenths.

We instinctively want to resolve dissonance. Our ears wince
at hearing the clash of notes that don't harmonize. We're emotionally, almost viscerally, on edge until the musical suspension
resolves. But consonant notes audibly "lock in" to one another.
And the contrast of harmony creates beauty.

It also gives context and indicates the direction of individual
notes. Play middle C on a piano, and on its own, the single note
doesn't tell you much about its place in the music. But play a
middle C in a chord, and it's surrounded with context, depth,

even illumination as to its purpose in a composition. Notes need one another.

If you've ever found yourself lost in the beauty of Pachelbel's "Canon in D," you've heard this play out. It's a simple melody, but it's surrounded by entire strands of corresponding melodies that weave in and out of one another. At times they intersect; at others they differ. But at every moment, they correlate to bring out a quality in the contrasting melody, one that produces an entirely different composition.

This is the theological significance of gender differences. Both male and female were intentionally created. Male and female are equal, independent expressions of their Composer. But together they create an *interdependent* harmony, one that correlates by design to underscore the differences between them. They are individual "notes" in an intricate composition. They give each other context and indicate direction. The harmony creates more than aesthetic beauty; it expresses the creative intent and will of the Composer. Like all works of art, we were designed to reflect a divine Artist. We are His creation. We receive our identity from Him.

## The Significance of Self-Giving

Contrary to the prevailing assumptions of our day, the meaning of sex and gender identity isn't found from within one's self but in relationship to another. John Finley describes sexual difference as an "irreducible otherness" that indicates "we are fulfilled not through self-absorption or self-expansion but through self-transcendence."[1] He states: "To find meaning in one's sex or gender identity solely from within the self is impossible. Sexuality reveals that we are profoundly structured for giving and receiving love on the level of the whole person."[2] It is inescapably relational.

The nature of sex and gender is self-giving and expressed relationally outside of ourselves. In other words, the significance of biological sex is discovered in our gendered relationships, and those gendered relationships are directed by our biological sex. Our sexed bodies indicate and inform our intended gender identities.

In his work *Theology of the Body*, John Paul II describes this relationship as "a communion of persons." The meaning of mankind as male and female is in their mutual self-giving, which mirrors God's own self-giving love. Their complementary bodies express that they are both gifts to each other.[3] In light of this, men and women cannot understand the meaning of their own identities apart from being in relationship: "Femininity is found in relation to masculinity and masculinity is confirmed in femininity. They depend on each other."[4]

Take away the fixed contrast between male and female, and we have no foundation to understand man or woman and even lose part of our understanding of God. Karl Barth described it this way: "It is always in relation to their opposite that man and woman are what they are in themselves."[5] Within the creation narrative, Dietrich Bonhoeffer saw human beings as a relational analogy, one that reflected the persons of the Godhead. The relationship between male and female personified the *imago Dei* in a way that neither could on their own.[6] I'd summarize it this way: male and female were created to depend on each other. Each was made to harmonize with the other, and neither can fully image God in isolation. The world needs both men and women to reflect what God is like. God created them to tell His story—to express His creative intent—better together.

Throughout the creation story, God arranges the physical world in a series of binaries: day and night. Earth and sky. Water and land. Sun and moon. And male and female.[7] "God establishes these binaries with boundaries that separate them, rulers who rule over them, and moral injunctions about what is to be done or avoided," explains Timothy Tennent in his work, *For the Body*.[8] Like the rest of God's creation, human beings have two forms. Yet unlike the rest of God's creation, they are "a little lower than the angels" (Ps. 8:5 KJV).

Humanity bears God's image. The theological term for this unique attribute of human beings is the *imago Dei*. There are many definitions for what it means to be the *imago Dei*. Some emphasize humanity's ability to be rational; others that humans are relational. John Kilner defines it as "reflection and connection."[9] Mankind was created to reflect God and have a special connection with God. We *bear* God's image. And as *bearers of* God's image, we belong to God Himself (Mark 12:16–17).

Male and female differences also reflect the complementary relationship between the two sexes. N. T. Wright connects the binaries of creation to the cosmic metanarrative—the complete, big-picture story—of God's relationship to humanity: "It's all about God making complementary pairs which are meant to work together. The last scene in the Bible is the new heaven and the new earth, and the symbol for that is the marriage of Christ and his church."[10] By complementary, I don't mean that male and female are opposites or completely different, but that they are structurally and relationally created for each other.[11] Brett McCracken compares this complementary difference to a lock and key. Separately, their differences are meaningless. But together, "their difference opens something up, unlocking something fuller and deeper about the human experience."[12]

Part of what makes the Christian sexual ethic so compelling is that it ascribes great meaning and significance to human sexuality *and* that this meaning and significance are not ultimate. Rather, they point to and reflect something even more transcendent than sexuality itself. Nancy Pearcey states, "What Christians do with their sexuality is one of the most important testimonies they give to the surrounding world."[13] Contrast ideas like "self-giving" and "communion of persons" and "otherness" with the way we usually hear gender identity described today. Terms like "my truth," "my authentic self," or "who I *really* am" characterize our culture's understanding of gender and its significance. The source of our identity and fulfillment is found almost exclusively in *self*, meaning the relationships in our lives ultimately exist to serve *self*. It's little wonder our society is so confused as to whether sex and gender have any deeper meaning. And it's little wonder so many find themselves suspended in relational dissonance, longing for the resolution that comes with self-giving harmony.

## Correlation and Contrast

The design for and meaning of sexual differentiation is imprinted on male and female bodies. Human beings are structured both for sexual reproduction and for relational communion. Abigail Favale describes how male and female are designed "purposefully to correspond to the difference of the other. . . . We are talking about a body that is designed to fit another kind of body, in an entirely unique way."[14] Sex differences are not accidental or incidental to our humanity. They are deeply embedded in our physical bodies. And this, like all of God's creation, is good.

Genesis 1 emphasizes the commonality between male and female. They are both in God's image and both personally created by Him. They are both commanded to rule and reign over creation, and are both part of the creation mandate to fill the earth with offspring. Verses 26–29 identify the first human beings with the Hebrew words *zakar* (male) and a *nequbah* (female). These terms depict their biological categories, specifically the sexual difference between male and female. Like the rest of creation, biological sex identity is determined by how an organism is constructed for sexual reproduction.[15] Males donate genetic material (impregnate); females receive and gestate genetic material (pregnancy).[16] The organization of male and female bodies reveals their respective reproductive contributions.

Our bodies are like physical signposts for the reality of our Creator God. He not only created them to be good; He created them to be a guide. They reveal order, purpose, and design. They teach us both individual identity *and* interdependence. Tennent describes the body as not just a biological category but a theological category, one that reveals God: "[T]he body makes the invisible mysteries of God's nature and redemption manifest and visible as a tangible marker in the world."[17] Sexual difference is neither accidental nor incidental to creation. It's an essential part of the goodness of God's design.

Genesis 1 reveals that sex difference is binary. Genesis 2 reveals that gender is also binary. Genesis 1 places male and female in relationship to the rest of God's creation. They are His image-bearing stewards of the physical world. Genesis 2 places male and female in relationship to each other. They have a unique relationship with God and with one another. In this poetic re-telling of the creation story, God is not called *Elohim* but His personal name, *Yahweh*. He personally forms the man and fashions the woman (*yatsar* and *banah*, respectively). Here humanity is no longer called *zakar* (male) and *nequbah* (female). Instead they are *ish* and *ishah*—man and woman. This pair of terms reflects how male and female *relate* to each other. Just as the woman came from the man, so *ishah* comes from *ish*; the word's origin reflects their relationship. In other words, *ish* and *ishah* describe their gender identity.

The Lord chose to create the man and the woman in different ways. He formed the man out of the dust of the earth (Gen. 2:8), but He fashioned the woman out of the side of the man (Gen. 2:18). He could have created the woman precisely the same way He created the man. That certainly would have conveyed their ontological equality. But instead, the Lord fashioned the woman out of the same substance as the man. The man immediately recognized and celebrated her identity for both communion and procreation: "Their difference is complementary," Favalae describes, "but asymmetrical. . . . She resembles him in their shared humanity . . . but differs in the feminine form of her humanity."[18] She was *of* him but *not* him. She was both a correlation and a contrast. They each fully possess the image of God individually, yet are incapable of fully manifesting it to the world apart from each other.

Note that we're talking about *men* and *women* here, not only husbands and wives. This does not mean a single woman is not fully made in God's image unless she gets married or that she can't reflect God without a husband. It means that we—God's masterpieces—cannot fulfill His purposes without both men and woman working together in the world interdependently, and that can happen in a variety of ways. Whether married or unmarried, the meaning and purpose of our embodied lives is found and directed outside of ourselves and in relationships.

The language of Genesis reveals another correlation, a new layer of harmony. This time not between the man and the woman relationally but within themselves personally. The pairs of terms in Genesis 1 and 2 correspond, confirming that both sex differences and gender differences were created to be binary. If a human being is a male (*zakar*), God created him to be a man (*ish*). If a human being is a female (*nequbah*), then God created her to be a woman (*ishah*). The sexed body was designed to correlate with the gendered self. By design, sex *indicates* and *informs* gender. Someone with a male anatomy is a man, and someone with a female anatomy is a woman. Biology indicates and informs identity. We can trust our bodies to tell us who we are.[19] Andrew Walker summed it up this way: "Our bodies do not lie to us."[20] Our gender is indeed more than our biology (a woman is a woman even after a hysterectomy, for example), but it isn't less. Our physical bodies represent our entire beings. We are not identified as a collection of individual parts but as a whole person. The sexed body is a created gift. God designed and bestowed it upon humanity in goodness and love.

Every aspect of our bodies has a purpose, including our reproductive anatomy. This refers to the *telos* (goal, fulfillment) of God's design. The purpose of the body is not only in reproductive function (Gen. 1:26–29) but also in personal relationships (Gen. 2:18–25). Maleness and femaleness have a purpose. The universe is not the product of blind determinism but a Designer who created man and woman to reflect a deeper meaning both individually and together.

## The Meaning of the Body

The opening words of Scripture reveal a Creator who is separate from, yet intimately involved in, His creation. This Creator God, *Elohim*, is infinite, but His creation is finite; He is self-sustaining, but His creation is contingent. Everything He makes—material and immaterial—is good. And everything He makes has order, purpose, and design.

Being made in the *imago Dei* encompasses our whole being. The image of God includes not only our immaterial selves (our minds, our souls, our relationships) but also our material selves. Various aspects of our humanity may be distinct (heart, conscience, flesh, etc.), but they are not divisible. We are complex, whole beings. Our physical selves reflect God. They are part of the *imago Dei*. They are essential and very good (Gen. 1:26–29). The human body has theological significance, revealing God's nature and design. Every part of the body has a function; every cell is complex. Like all of God's creation, our bodies have order, purpose, and design. They reveal His nature, His attributes, and His covenantal love (Rom. 1:20–21).[21] Scripture places a high value on the human body.[22]

In the early days of the church, Christianity's view of the body stood out among the pagan religions. To the Greco-Roman world, it would have been foolish, even scandalous. Ancient society was brimming with philosophies that despised the body. Philosophical systems like Platonism, Gnosticism, and Manicheanism held that the physical world was evil. Living in a body was like a descent of the soul from the "higher spiritual realm into the corrupt material realm"; it was a place of "death, decay, and destruction."[23] The point of the body was to be a "container" for the soul.[24]

Nancy Pearcey describes just how much the ancients detested the physical world. Ancient Gnosticism taught the lowest of the gods (who was really an evil subdeity) was responsible for creating the material world. The higher gods wanted nothing to do with the physical world: "After all, no self-respecting god would demean himself by mucking about with matter."[25] The physical world was evil. The goal of your soul—your inner self, your *true* self—was to escape it.

Into this cultural environment, where the material world is belittled and the immaterial world is exalted, Christianity bursts with the proclamation that the one true God created the physical world and that it was good (Gen. 1). The Creator Himself came to His creation in bodily form (Heb. 2:13).[26] As God incarnate, He willingly involved Himself in the physical world. Not only that, but the God-Man, Jesus, was bodily resurrected. He wasn't "psychologically resurrected" in the hearts and minds of His disciples. He was physically raised. And Jesus didn't try to escape the material world after His death so He could float on a cloud somewhere; He *returned* to it (1 Cor. 15:3; Rev. 22:20). Even more, when the resurrected Lord ascended to the Father, He retained His bodily form. Thus, redeemed, physical humanity has been introduced to the highest place of goodness, the unrestrained presence of God (Mark 16:19). Finally, at the culmination of human history, the Lord will physically return in bodily form. Since Jesus is the Forerunner to His followers, they will share in His physical resurrection with renewed bodies, like His own. In fact, they are called the "body of Christ" (Rom. 7:4; 1 Cor. 10:16; 12:27; Eph. 4:12)). The body is deeply significant to our Creator God.

The Bible gives our bodies profound dignity and inherent worth: we cannot regard the *imago Dei* and disregard our physical, embodied selves.[27] At times, Christian history has adopted some of the Greek dualism between the body and the soul. But Scripture reveals the two as inseparable. They are two sides of the same coin.[28] When we die, we are "absent from the body," but even this is temporary and incomplete (2 Cor. 5:8), what Christian tradition calls the "intermediate state." Our soul's destination includes being reunited with a redeemed, resurrected body.[29] "The gospel message is that the entire physical world will be transformed," Nancy Pearcey explains. "Humans will not be saved *out of* the material creation but will be saved *together with* the material creation."[30] Embodied, physical existence is the fullness and future of humanity.

Our culture's distrust of the body may seem novel. But it's just a new expression of an old idea. Gender ideology claims the "physical you" is a prison the "authentic you" must escape. Who you *truly* are is different from your body.[31] It alienates the biological self from the gendered self. Take away the terms and technology we use today, and we're left with a new version of ancient Gnosticism and Greek dualism.

## The De-meaning of the Body

To sever gender identity from biological sex robs the body of its theological meaning and its inherent worth. Apart from a God-centered view of our physical selves, the only meaning our physical bodies have is what we choose to give them. Or, as feminist author Camilla Paglia summed it up: "Fate, not God, has given us this flesh. We have absolute claim to our bodies and may do with them as we see fit."[32] When our embodied selves are stripped of meaning, when we don't allow them to define or direct our gender identity, then our own goal or fulfillment for our gender—our own personal *telos*—is no longer self-giving. Instead, it becomes self-actualizing.

The harmony between Genesis 1 and 2 shows the harmony God intended between sex and gender. The body is not merely a collection of bones and organs, muscles and nerves. It has intrinsic theological meaning and purpose. And we cannot separate our bodies from our identities.

Trans ideologies disconnect the outer body from the inner self. The body and the self are not just *distinct* but *divisible* aspects of human identity. But they also separate the body from its purpose. By severing the physical self from the gendered self, they deprive the body of the theological meaning God bestowed upon it.[33] And, consequently, they overlook the good, loving Creator who made us with order, purpose, and design. Favale believes the concept of gender has driven a "wedge" between body and identity. Biological sex used to reference a fact of nature. But gender ideology diminishes, even decimates, the body's role in establishing identity. As a result, no one seems to know what gender really is: "Separated from the body, gender becomes impossible to identify." As gender becomes disconnected from sex, our society has "an even more fragmented and unstable understanding of personhood."[34] In Pearcey's words, the transgender narrative is "radically dehumanizing." It alienates a person from her body while the Christian worldview honors the body as part of our fully integrated identity.[35]

## Gender Dysphoria and the Christian Worldview

Considering this, how should we theologically respond to someone struggling with gender dysphoria or someone who has undergone a gender transition? How do we "speak the truth in love" in a world that interprets speaking the truth as hateful and bigoted (Eph. 4:15)?

Let's think theologically together and apply the Christian worldview to these questions. This is by no mean comprehensive, and I hope you'll add more detail to it yourself. But when we consider gender identity through the Christian perspectives of creation, fall, and redemption, we'll discover a framework that enables us to understand and respond with both truth and love.

## Creation

God created humanity to be either male or female. Sex and gender are aspects of our human nature that He sovereignly gives. The purpose of sex and gender is to reflect and image God Himself in a manner unique to the rest of creation. The human body is good. Since we are God's creations and sexuality is a gift from Him, God alone has the authority to define how we should live and use His gifts. Sprinkle captures the connection between who we were created to be and how we were created to live: "We need to first understand who we *are* (ontology) before we know what it means to become who God wants us to *be* (discipleship). Ontology is integral to discipleship, because discipleship means living as we were designed to live—living as divine images."[36]

Since God has created us to be complex, whole beings, it's impossible to divide sex from gender. Thus, the issue of gender incongruence is an issue of ontology, or what it means to be human.[37] Gender is not the end-all, be-all to determine our identity, but it is a created manifestation of our identity as the *imago Dei*. Since we are immersed in a cultural mindset that separates the sexed body from the gendered self, it's all the more important that we are clear and consistent. We will never understand the meaning and significance of our sexed bodies or our gendered selves apart from acknowledging the reality of our Creator. Following God's design for our lives, specifically our genders and sexualities, is for our good and to protect us from the self-inflected damage that disobedience brings.

## The Fall

Because of human sinfulness, the beauty of sexuality has been distorted. God's good gift is misused as a source and cause of pain, brokenness, and depravity. Our culture's view of gender may be new to us, but it's as old as Genesis 3.

In his book *Live No Lies*, pastor John Mark Comer summarizes the deception of sin and why we fall for it so easily: "We sin because we believe a lie about what will make us happy."[38] Listen to the stories of transgender people, and you'll hear this as a running theme. In a myriad of ways, we reprise the scenario of Genesis 3, believing we can take authority from God and "redefine good and evil based on the voice in our heads and the inclination of our hearts, rather than trust in the loving word of God."[39]

Underneath the psychological, sociological, and philosophical explanations for the transgender epidemic lies a spiritual deception. And we are living in a spiritual battle, one in which Satan—the enemy of God and all God loves—seeks to kill, steal, and destroy (John 10:10). He has one strategy and a thousand different tactics to fulfill it: He lies. He deceives. He blinds us to the truth (2 Cor. 4:4). "The devil's primary stratagem to drive the soul and society into ruin is *deceptive ideas that play to disordered desires*."[40] Comer describes the devil's deception: "You're not just a human being with a place in an ordered cosmos over creation but still under the Creator. No, you can transgress your limitations and become whoever and whatever you want. Identity is self-defined. Morality is self-determined. Take control of your own life. 'You will be like God.'"[41] It is both the lure of self-fulfillment and the lull of self-delusion.

God calls His children to be different, separate, and set apart from the surrounding world—what Scripture calls holiness. The call to holiness transforms every aspect and season of life. But sexuality is often where the people of God most boldly contrast their culture. Comer identifies three reasons for this: first, sexuality is "the primary test of our generation's fidelity to the Way of Jesus or to the world's ideas and ideologies." It is the central battleground for our affections, commitments, and identities. Second, sexuality was "one of *the* most common New Testament examples of non-Christian behavior." In fact, twisting doctrine to justify sexual sin was a mark of false teaching. And third, "sexuality has always been an arena where followers of Jesus stand in sharp contrast to the world. From the acropolis of Athens to the sidewalks of Brooklyn."[42] The Christian sexual ethic runs counter to every other worldview's claims about human dignity and sexuality.

Some Christians support the transition of those who suffer from gender dysphoria. I believe they have good intentions: mercy seeks to alleviate the painful effects of our broken world. But if there's anything I hope you discovered in the previous pages, it's that gender transition methods will further alienate gender-confused people not only from their own bodies but also from the truth, and may even worsen their condition. If we are truly advocating for the good of those afflicted with gender dysphoria, we cannot support measures, however temporary, that add to their harm. If we long to see our gender-dysphoric neighbor live as God designed—which includes finding harmony within their body, we risk implicitly contributing to self-estrangement when we support or affirm gender transition.

Our identity is theologically bestowed; we don't create it from within ourselves. We receive it from God, who created us for Himself, to reflect Himself. In light of this, we must recognize gender transition is not God's best or His design for His image bearers. Thus, we must categorize gender transition as a move against God and His ways. We all sin and fall short of God's glory. Gender transition is among the many ways human beings try to live apart from God's design to misuse the good gifts He's given us. I like how Andrew Walker says it: "We all coerce ourselves in a direction that runs against nature each time we seek to sit on God's throne."[43]

I'm deeply aware that no one *chooses* the anguish of gender dysphoria. And the last thing I want to do is add to anyone's pain. But in a time of continuous and contagious confusion, it's important that we're clear about *what* the affliction of gender dysphoria is if we are to offer any hope of healing: gender dysphoria is a psychological condition in which one's mind and body are out of alignment. To someone with gender dysphoria, none of this may sound like good news. It might even sound like abstract theological claims that forget about actual people (although I hope that's not the case).

I'm not a counselor, a psychologist, or a medical doctor. I obviously can't give you medical or psychological advice. But I can tell you, based on all the facts—and how they prove the teachings of the Christian Scriptures—that every human being was created by God as male or female by design and that the alienation and self-loathing of gender dysphoria requires a healing deeper than any surgeon can reach. We all have a real need for peace. But acting on the desire to live as the opposite gender by rejecting how God created us and living outside His design won't bring peace.[44] Going against God's design never does.

Our fallen world, the enemy of our souls, and our own sinful hearts constantly work to deceive us, to convince us that anything *other* than God's ways will fulfill and free us. Gender ideology and its beliefs about our humanity are no exception. A gender-dysphoric person's desire to remedy her broken condition is real. We instinctively feel the effects of the fall. We know our relationships with others and even ourselves are not all they should be. And in this, a trans person has found part of the truth—she needs to be remade. She does indeed need to be a new person, just not in the way she thought. She does need to find peace and wholeness, but not through the strategies presented to her. And she can't attain it on her own.

## Redemption

Gender dysphoria is not a sin. Read that again. If someone is suffering from acute mental distress, she is suffering the effects of a feeling. And feelings are usually symptoms. That doesn't mean they're insignificant. Far from it. Just think about the way anxiety or fear creeps up in your own life. Symptoms are good in that they reveal something not as it ought to be. They help alert us to something amiss, something that needs attention. But the presence of gender dysphoria—whether among the rare cases of persistent dysphoria beginning in early childhood or among the rapid-onset cases troubling countless teens and young adults— isn't a sin.[45] In most cases it's a symptom.

Gender dysphoria is also a form of suffering. This suffering can be a result of someone's choices, or how someone else's choices affect us, or simply because we live in a broken world. In one way that might not sound very hopeful. Until we remember what God says about suffering. God never wastes our pain, including the pain of gender dysphoria. In his book *Walking with God through Pain and Suffering*, pastor Tim Keller says that some suffering "has no purpose other than to lead a person to love God more ardently for himself alone and so discover the ultimate peace and freedom."[46] Our emotional and psychological struggles can be tools in God's hand in the shaping of our souls. And this will outlast every affliction and pain and confusion and heartache heaped upon us in this life.

When Paul said he'd found the secret to contentment, he was sitting in house arrest and dependent on friends to bring him food. More than that, he had *finally* made it to Rome—the deepest longing of his heart—and what happens when he gets there? He's arrested. How did he learn contentment in suffering? It wasn't emptying himself of his desires or longings. It's that he'd already gained the one thing worth getting in this world, the only thing that would outlast everything else: Christ. And because he had Christ, whatever struggle he endured took on a different perspective. The greatest sufferings he faced were tools of his all-loving, all-powerful, all-wise God, who had already predetermined how He would use those struggles for Paul's eternal gain (Phil. 1–4).

Jesus referred to this as carrying our cross. Different people are called to carry different crosses at different times in their lives. But they all have two things in common. First, each cross requires its bearer to deny herself. "To carry a cross," Walker describes, "means to deny ourselves—to lose whatever defined and directed our lives before we met our Maker."[47] Second, each cross is given to its recipient. It's not like we get to pick it out of a catalog. Implicit in carrying a cross is trusting that the God who loves us has both allowed it and predestined it for our ultimate good (Rom. 8:28).

Our hopeful expectation in suffering goes beyond the question of whether it will go away—our fallen, post-Genesis 3 world is full of pain. Rather, our hope is that the God who Himself suffered on our behalf will, one day, redeem and restore everything this fallen world affects; and—in the meantime—He will cause every trial to work for our ultimate good. The Suffering Servant transforms our sufferings into our servants.

The weight of gender incongruence is a heavy burden. To look in the mirror and feel you were born in the wrong body, to sense foreboding clouds of depression form as you long to be and look like and live as the opposite gender, to freeze with anxiety in front of public restrooms not knowing which one you should enter. I can't imagine the pain. And I won't pretend to know what that's like.

But I do know what it is to carry a cross I didn't choose, not knowing if it will ever change, to wonder why God seems to close His ears to the deepest cries of my soul, to pray with tears in my eyes and sense heaven's answer is simply to be faithful as and where I am.

I wish our trials came with expiration dates printed on them, like orange juice or yogurt. Then we'd know just how long we have to learn whatever we need to learn from them and move on. But God doesn't give us that. And the truth is, some of us will struggle for our entire lives with what Paul called "a thorn in the flesh." It does indeed have an expiration date—one day every pain will be healed (Rev. 21:4). But, for now, we're caught in the "in between," the "How long, O Lord?," and the "Will this ever go away?"

God can answer our prayers, both the wails and the whispers. And He can take away our pain, however crushing its weight or piercing its ache. In the blink of an eye He could do it. And in many cases, He's done that for some people with agonizing inner struggles. But God can also use our pain to give us what we don't even know we need and to shape us into something greater than we can possibly see right now. Sometimes the greatest act of faith is quietly believing that the One who is all-loving and all-powerful is also all-wise. We may never understand why we go through what we go through. And some things won't make sense until we see Him face-to-face (1 Cor. 13:12). That's okay. He doesn't ask us to understand. He calls us to trust, to follow, to love, and to rest in Him. He'll take care of everything else (Ps. 138:8)

Healing will likely be a long road. The beliefs and behavior leading to trans identity are deeply rooted. There is no "snapping out of it." But as the testimonies of Christians who detransitioned show, the Holy Spirit *will* be faithful to lead, convict, and direct a transgender person to align with her biological sex *as a result* of her conversion and increasing discipleship. Note: A *result of* . . . not *a condition of*. There's a world of difference between a heart that is willing to follow Jesus with everything, but overwhelmed by the prospect of detransitioning, and an unyielding heart that justifies continuing in a transgender life.

We struggle in holiness as members of the body of Christ, indeed, members of one another (Rom. 12:5). No one should suffer from gender incongruence alone. We were made for deep, authentic connections, and those connections help form our own sense of identity. Christian communities will need patience, understanding, and grace to walk with those in their spiritual and emotional recovery. The Christian contending with gender dysphoria deserves complete inclusion in the house of God, a place of service and contribution, a place to belong and to be known. Keep in mind, the LGBTQIA+ community is a *community*, and they often rival the church in their expressions of love and hospitality.

## Conclusion

The created harmony between male and female runs from the first to the last moments of human history. The Christian worldview offers a fully integrated identity, one in which our sexed body has intrinsic purpose and worth and our gendered self has transcendent significance.[48] In all the factors that influence female identity, only one ascribes meaning. Female identity is theologically bestowed, a gift from the God who created it to reflect the wonder and depth of Himself. Apart from a reconciled relationship with our Creator, we will never comprehend, much less fulfill, the significance of our sexed bodies or our gendered selves.

# CHAPTER 6

# Around the Corner: What You Can't Afford Not to Know

*M* *om and Dad, I need to tell you I'm not actually a girl.* When twelve-year-old Grace came out to her parents as trans, they were shocked and shaken.[1] They knew their daughter had been attending a progressive public school. But Grace had a solid biblical foundation at home. Despite her outspoken affirmation that God made people male or female just months earlier, she assumed a nonbinary identity. In response, her teachers and classmates had "reeducated" her, inviting her to the school's Gender and Sexualities Alliance club, where she listened to other children and teens talk about how uncomfortable they were in their own bodies. Grace, whose autism spectrum disorder contributed to her vulnerability,[2] found she could relate. She saw the hyper-sexualized way other girls dressed and didn't want anything to do with it. In her mind, womanhood became synonymous with sexualization.

After coming out as trans, she received congratulations and approval. She was instantly accepted. Grace continued to assume the paradigm now so familiar with gender ideology: "People were so obsessed with victimhood. . . . I started telling people about the tiny sliver of Jewish I have in me because I wanted to be anything other than white." She wanted to dress like a boy, adopt a new nickname, and be called by masculine pronouns.

Grace's parents took drastic steps. Recovering their daughter from the influence of gender ideology was like rescuing a loved one from a cult. Her self-perception had to be deconstructed from false beliefs, then reconstructed with truth. It took physically removing her from the influence, building healthy relationships within their family, and engaging her with questions that required critical thought. Her parents wisely pulled her out of that public school. Recovery was slow, full of progress and setbacks. But eventually, God—through the love and faithfulness of her parents—led Grace back to identifying with the gender He'd given her.

Grace eventually desisted in her trans identity. Her recovery is a success story. It's a testament to the hope of transformation from the Spirit of truth and to the influence of identity formation in family relationships. But it's also proof that, however strong a young woman's biblical and spiritual foundation may be, she is still vulnerable to the cultural messages about sex and gender that inundate our world.

As we prepare for more girls like Grace in our families, churches, and communities, we must also prepare to respond to issues. Some of these are a matter of raising awareness—you can't respond to or prepare for something you don't know exists. But others are questions upon which theologically sound, spiritually mature believers have different views, and this requires us to walk in wisdom and sensitivity to God's Spirit and in charitable grace toward those who disagree.

## Rethinking Roles

Trans ideologies typically rest on gendered cultural expressions as proof of gender identity. The stereotypes become the substance. Christians who overemphasize gender differences and roles can fall into the same error. In Pearcey's words, "We must take care not to add to Scripture by baptizing gender expectations that are in reality historically contingent and arbitrary. . . . The church should be the first place where young people can find freedom from unbiblical stereotypes—the freedom to work out what it means to be created in God's image as holistic and redeemed people."[3] We must not reduce the complexity of our humanity to culturally defined expressions of gender. And we must not reduce Christian discipleship to a preoccupation with or precision over gender-specific commands.

Much of the evangelical gender debate in recent decades has centered on gender roles. The result has been, at times, an overemphasis on gender expressions and behaviors. We would do well to shift our focus to the relational character of gender differences established at creation, to allow for individual personalities and interests to develop, and to guide the formation of gender identity in the context of the whole body of Christ, recognizing the ways we reflect our Creator through differing responsibilities and relationships.

Scripture presents us with a holistic life, one in which our physical, relational, and spiritual selves are fully integrated. "Men aren't commanded to be masculine, and women aren't commanded to be feminine. They're both just commanded to be godly," Preston Sprinkle states.[4] When men and women follow the Bible's gender-specific commands as part of the whole-person discipleship of following the way of Jesus, they will embody and express the meaning of manhood and womanhood. In other words, the gender-specific commands shouldn't comprise the totality of what a man or a woman is taught about the Bible. The whole Bible is for the whole person, and only when one is following the whole counsel of Scripture will its gender-specific commands make any sense. Focus on the whole Bible, and you'll get a whole person as a result, living out what it means to be a woman or a man as God designed.

## Social Spaces

Ask gender activists about transgender rights, and admittance of trans women to female social spaces is almost representative of the issue. With good reason—biological males in women's spheres generate some of the greatest shock, indignation, and concern for women's well-being. Attorneys Alessandra Asteriti and Rebecca Bull argue "gender self-declaration" harms women's rights. To acknowledge a woman's "bodily integrity and autonomy" requires that she would have the liberty to "choose to exclude a male (regardless of gender identity) from female-only spaces." A female should be free to "withhold consent" to share intimate spaces with individuals she perceives to be male.[5]

Some implications concern female equality and privacy: high school female athletes get elbowed out of scholarship opportunities when their school required they compete against males; males with negligible rankings against other males shattered records by several seconds after moving to the women's division. Retailers like Target, Starbucks, and Barnes & Noble announced they welcome trans customers to choose the bathroom corresponding with their gender identity.

Other implications concern female vulnerability and safety. A thirtysomething entered a women's spa changing room dressed as a woman and exposed his erect penis to an underage girl.[6] Trans women have impregnated and sexually assaulted female inmates in women's prisons.[7] Social spaces like bathrooms, locker rooms, domestic violence shelters, rape refuges, and even prisons are the spheres in which these public debates play out.[8]

For many genuinely gender-dysphoric people, choosing between a men's and a women's restroom is fraught with intense social anxiety. A female who presents as a man may feel out of place in a women's room but physically vulnerable in a men's room. She's not trying to make a statement. She's just trying to use the bathroom. She may even be in such a vulnerable state that socially participating as a female can add to her distress or trigger an impulse to self-harm. In our awareness of transgender issues, we must not abandon our responsibility to care for transgender people. Preston Sprinkle's *Embodied* and Andrew Walker's *God and the Transgender Debate* both address practical questions like bathrooms, sleeping spaces, and summer camps with consistency and sensitivity. I recommend both works for you to consider and implement as the Spirit leads you.

## The Poison of Porn

It's impossible to discuss transgender culture without noting the threefold poison of pornography. First, many girls who declare themselves trans have viewed violent pornographic material at a young age. Pornography has terrified young women about the idea of having sex with a man. Among sexually active girls between fourteen and seventeen years old, some 13 percent report being choked during sexual activity.[9] One therapist whose practice works with a large number of trans-identifying adolescents shared that her young patients are "often pretty freaked out by porn. . . . In some cases, porn played a big role in their new adopted identity."[10]

Second, many gender-dysphoric males exhibit a psychological condition called autogynephilia. The term means "love of one's self as a woman." Autogynephilic men are often sexually attracted to women but experience sexual arousal at the fantasy or act of looking like a woman. One of the most well-known cases of autogynephilia was Einar Wegener/Lili Elbe, whose story was portrayed in the 2015 film *The Danish Girl*. Autogynephilia is proliferated by a genre of pornography known as "sissy porn," in which the "women" portrayed are feminized men coerced into sexual submission, fetishizing their humiliation. Many "sissy porn" videos also tell male viewers that they are, and always have been, women and that, just by watching, they have participated in a sexually submissive act.[11] It's dark and demonic. And it's easily accessible to children and teens. Parents, ministers, and counselors need to be aware of this to know what questions to ask: Is the gender-dysphoric adolescent using gender as a coping mechanism for another source of pain, or have they been exposed to pornographic material that has infected the mind? To neglect this distinction will cause us to conflate the two issues unfairly. The two conditions are not the same.

Third, trans-identifying teens are extremely vulnerable to being victimized by the porn industry. A gender-dysphoric teen may find her family relationships and social support networks disrupted or broken down. The only welcoming environment is among others in the LGBTQIA+ community. Many become homeless and even more vulnerable to prostitution. "Transgender youth cannot be left unsupported by family and church to figure out how to become a young adult while left in the hands of unloving strangers and predators."[12] Transgender porn is one of the most viewed pornographic categories. PornHub reported searches for transgender porn quadrupled between 2014 and 2017, and "trans" was the fifth highest search term in 2018.[13] Transgender adolescents and young adults, isolated from the emotional and spiritual support of those seeking their well-being, can quickly become exploited for paraphilic purposes.[14]

## The Education System

As Grace's story reveals, public schools are becoming laboratories for gender ideology. Public school teachers openly post on social media how they are influencing young students to embrace gender ideologies. One preschool teacher, Koe Creation, celebrated how the three- to five-year old children in her class understood and reiterated her gender theories: "Today at the lunch table, when the topic of gender and genitals came up, one of our students plainly looked up and said, 'Well, I'm a girl today, but I know that teacher Koe isn't. No, they're NB [nonbinary].'"[15] Another nonbinary teacher explains how three-year-olds are capable of understanding gender identity, sexual orientation, and pronouns.[16]

Elementary school children are also taught "The Genderbread Person," which explains the differences between sexual anatomy, sexual attraction, gender identity, and gender expression. The Gingerbread Person's brain, heart, and genitals comprise different aspects of his or her overall identity and do not need to align with one gender or another.[17] Or, as we said before, the inner self and the outer self are severed from each other, and the physical body is just a collection of parts.

In California, gender-identity instruction occurs in kindergarten.[18] The state's guidelines claim: "While students may not fully understand the concepts of gender expression and identity, some children in kindergarten and even younger have identified as transgender or understand they have a gender identity that is different from their sex assigned at birth." The law forbids parents from objecting to the state's gender education program. While they can opt out of sexual health lessons that discuss sexual organs and their functions, parents may not remove their children from lessons on gender identity.

As of July 2020, Illinois joined California, Colorado, New Jersey, and Oregon in requiring public schools to teach LGBTQ history and purchase textbooks that include the topic. Education curriculum introduces three-year-olds to the meaning of *lesbian*, *gay*, and *transgender*. Training material also features a teacher reading from *I Am Jazz*, a children's book describing the experiences of a transgender child, explaining to preschoolers that being transgender means "having a girl brain but a boy body" and looking at the camera to tell children they, too, "can be just like Jazz."[19]

Pre-K and elementary school teachers share their excitement over their free book bundles from Pride and Less Prejudice, a children's book publisher emphasizing gender education.[20] Topics include exploring same-sex feelings in friendship, nonbinary identities, same-sex parents, transgender siblings, and discovering whether you're transgender. Young, impressionable minds learn about *Jack (Not Jackie)*, where a big sister realizes her little sister prefers playing in the mud over wearing dresses and is really "Jack"; or *Sparkle Boy*, where little Casey learns to proudly wears his painted nails, shimmery skirt, and sparkly bracelet outside around all the other kids; or *Worm Loves Worm*, where two worms fall in love and get married, but their friends ask which one will wear the dress and which one will wear the tux, but eventually learn it doesn't matter, because the worms love each other. Targeted age groups for Pride and Less Prejudice books are Pre-K to third grade, and first to fifth grade.

Teachers may or may not inform parents when their child declares a trans identity or socially transitions. A Los Angeles mom filed suit against her school district after claiming her eleven-year-old daughter's teacher manipulated her into a gender transition and "drove a wedge between mother and child" by hiding it from the family.[21] In Pittsburgh, three parents allege their children's first grade teacher introduced their children to gender dysphoria by reading trans-themed children's books and telling them sometimes "parents are wrong" about gender.[22]

A North Carolina preschool teacher resigned after using LGBTQ-themed flashcards to teach her students about colors. The flashcards included a "Progress Pride Flag" and a pregnant man.[23] A lesson for first graders titled "Pink, Blue, and Purple," from the gender curriculum *Rights, Respect, Responsibility*, introduces children to gender fluidity.[24] The six- and seven-year-olds are told they know and feel their gender identity, no matter what their biology:

> Identity starts with an I. . . . You might feel like
> you are a boy, you might feel like you are a girl.
> You might feel like you're a boy even if you have
> body parts that some people might tell you are
> "girl" parts. You might feel like you're a girl even

if you have body parts that some people might
tell you are "boy" parts. And you might not feel
like you're a boy or a girl, but you're a little bit
of both. No matter how you feel, you're perfectly
normal![25]

The K-12 program, produced by Advocates for Youth, has
been adapted for and implemented in several states, including
Florida, Colorado, Maryland, Washington, New Jersey, and
Louisiana.

## Seize the Smartphone

Neurologist Frances Jensen has studied adolescent brain
development. She found teenage brains were more highly
impressionable than adult brains.[26] Teens are also more prone
to developing addictions, a vulnerability caused by incomplete
brain development. The frontal lobe of the brain, which controls
decision-making, is not fully insulated by a protective material
called myelin until a person's mid- to late twenties. The result
is an adolescent who is especially moody, impulsive, and not yet
adept at responsible decision-making, especially decisions that
involve risk.

Jensen connects this to teen social media use and the
"wealth of new stimuli" a girl can access before her internal judg-
ment has fully formed. She may not know how to assess whether
certain information is safe or how watching a video will affect
her long after she views it. "They are unaware of when to gate
themselves," she explains. Because of the adolescent's developmental stage, addictions are even more difficult to break among
teens than among adults.[27] "The brain," Jensen explains, "is a
product of both nature and nurture, including all the exposures,

stresses, and stimulations of a person's environment. . . . What we learn and experience, the good and the bad, the mild to the severe, will change our brains."[28]

The combination of emotional vulnerability and social media use among young women is like the ascent of a roller coaster. It reaches a tipping point before dropping adolescent girls into the confusion of ROGD and pulling them ever further like a centripetal force. Before Keira Bell transitioned at sixteen, she found gender ideology online. At thirteen, Grace Lidinsky-Smith discovered online friends via Tumblr who diagnosed her depression as trans identity. Helena Kirschner, also a detransitioner, described social media as "an all-day alternate reality escape from the real world."[29] Just search for "top surgery" on TikTok, currently the most popular social media platform among teens, and you'll find pro-trans videos with millions of views.[30] Smartphones and social media are forming adolescents in a myriad of ways. There's a reason Silicon Valley billionaires forbid or highly restrict screen time for their own children.[31]

## What's in a Name . . . or a Pronoun?

Should Christians use preferred pronouns? Because we don't have an explicit command in Scripture, we must grapple with its implications and be led by the Spirit. Godly, thoughtful believers have arrived at different conclusions on this question.

On one side of the conversation, you'll find purehearted, theologically sound believers who refuse to call a trans person by her preferred pronouns in an effort to be clear and uncompromising in the truth. Proponents of this view often say something like they don't want to lie to a transgender person or to participate in what they believe is wrong. They may also refuse to submit to "compelled speech," especially speech that violates one's conscience.[32] The mother of a gender-dysphoric teen girl refused to use her daughter's preferred pronouns: "I would have to choose between offending God or offending you." Her response directed her daughter back to her Creator with clarity and certainty. It also helped reframe gender identity away from confused and transient feelings and recentered it on a created identity.

On the other end of the debate, you'll also find purehearted, theologically sound believers who do use preferred pronouns in an effort to be loving, kind, and even evangelistic. Proponents of this view often talk about meeting trans people where they are and avoiding the loss of rapport that comes with refusal. Why waste the opportunity of speaking into someone's life because you disagree with how they view themselves? They may also consider that some gender-dysphoric people are provoked to harm themselves when they hear biologically based pronouns. This approach is often called "pronoun hospitality," in which the Christian will do what is personally uncomfortable to maintain the opportunity for influence and, eventually, sharing the gospel.

A third approach centers on the relationship you have with the transgender person as well as the trans person's own relationship to the truth. Pastor Sam Allberry says there are times to use preferred pronouns and other times to avoid them. With a trans person he just met, he would practice pronoun hospitality and seek to help the individual arrive at the truth. But with a gender-dysphoric teenager in his church who already knows the truth, he would refuse.[33] Knowing the difference requires sensitivity to the Spirit.

Each of these views attempts to navigate a difficult cultural moment and a delicate interaction with a potentially fragile person. Each is admirable, even noble. But we may be missing an important element in this conversation. Our culture approaches concepts like "woman" and "man" as self-imposed categories. They are "language-based identities" that anyone can inhabit at will. Words aren't just words. Within gender ideology, language doesn't reflect reality; it *creates* reality.[34] The tenderhearted Christian's sensitivity to a transgender person may be misconstrued as affirming a belief that is fundamentally at odds with the truth about God, humanity, and reality.

My personal approach? Call the person by his or her preferred name, but avoid the pronouns. You typically can. Should the conversation arise, share your convictions in a spirit of gentleness: while you don't intend to give offense, you believe God created every person in love and in His image, that our maleness or femaleness isn't an accident or a mistake but part of how we reflect and know our Creator. Also, consider the gender-confused people in your family, circle of friends, or congregations. What might the use of preferred pronouns convey to them? Will it contribute to a teenager's confusion? What about someone who comes to Christ and, in their discipleship, has detransitioned back to living according to her biological sex? As we consider how best to respond to the spiritual needs of the trans community, we can't forget those who are already in our spiritual care. First Corinthians 10 describes how we will come to varying conclusions on cultural questions. We all must do what accords with our conscience and considers others. So, wherever you land and whatever you conclude, practice it out of conviction, not fear.

While we're on the subject of preferred pronouns, let's talk about Christians volunteering their own. Some believers, out of a desire to reach and connect with the LGBTQ community, introduce themselves with or publicly post their own preferred pronouns. However well-intended, I believe that's a mistake. And it's one you can easily avoid. When David Sanchez, who serves as a director of ethics and justice, is asked to give his pronouns, he replies, "I want you to get to know me, not make any assumptions. First and foremost, my identity is in Christ." When Andrew Walker, a professor of ethics, gets the question, he responds, "Out of respect for my own conscience and views on the matter, I'm going to refrain from stating my pronouns. But I'm otherwise very excited to be here today and look forward to our meeting."[35] Or there's always the tongue-in-cheek version: "I identify as someone who does not use preferred pronouns." (You might want to read the room before you pull that one.) Offering your preferred pronouns goes beyond "pronoun hospitality" for others who struggle with gender confusion. In my view, it's entering into and participating in a philosophy that separates the body from the self.

Before we leave the topic of language, let's consider the phrase "trans Christian." For some believers, the phrase functions as a type of "shorthand." They are Christians who are walking in step with God's design, but their gender dysphoria still lingers. But others use the phrase to convey something different, namely that trans identity harmonizes with their Christian discipleship. The phrase can be confusing. But even more than that, it's a disservice to Christians who are faithfully following Jesus while they bear the suffering of gender dysphoria. If we are in Christ, we are not identified by our past sins or present struggles. In 1 Corinthians 6, Paul describes sins that cut us off from God, among them sexual sins. He states, "Such *were* some of you" (v. 11 KJV, emphasis added). Redemption includes being saved from every departure from God's ways, whether because of deception or outright disobedience. And it comes with a new identity. In a culture that fixates on SOGI as the all-important aspect of our identities, choosing not to label or modify our Christian identity is a declaration. It tells a confused and sin-captive world that we are no longer defined by our struggles. In fact, we are "more than conquerors" over them through Christ who loved us (Rom. 8:37). Language matters. And how we describe ourselves and others should reflect our identity as children of our God, not orphans of our culture.

## Family Rights

Finally, detaching biology from gender dismantles the foundation for family relationships. As the government continues to enshrine gender ideology within education and law, the state will incrementally replace the role and rights of parents. The human being who birthed you isn't a "mother"; she's your "gestational parent," the female whose birth canal you exited. The "penis-having human" who sired you isn't a father; he's an "inseminator" who donated sperm to your "birthing person."

Stella Morabito predicted this after the Obama administration's transgender bathroom directive in 2016. By prioritizing gender identity over biological sex, our society has effectively become "sexless." The sexed body no longer matters in language or law. When a state abolishes biological distinctions between male and female in its laws, it can also abolish recognition of biological ties among families and regulate family relationships. "In a society de-sexed by law, would the state recognize your relationship as a husband or a wife? Mother or father? Daughter or son? Those are all sexed terms," she explains. "A system that does not recognize the existence of male and female would be free to ignore the parentage of any child. You might be recognized as your child's 'legal guardian,' but only if the state agrees to that. Anybody can be a guardian to your child if the state decides it's in the child's 'best interest.'"[36]

Nancy Pearcey echoes this warning and calls the elimination of gendered family terms a "power grab" by the state. In the past, the government recognized marriage as a "pre-political right," since human beings are a sexually reproducing species. The state acknowledged, but did not confer, the right to marriage. The same concept applies to family and personhood. By removing biology as a relevant factor in one's identity and relationships, the state recognizes them as emotional commitments. "The only way the law can treat a trans woman (born male) the same as a biological woman is to deny the relevance of biology and declare gender to a matter of inner feelings. . . . Pre-political rights are being reduced to merely legal rights at the dispensation of the state. And what the state gives, it can take away. Human rights are no longer inalienable."[37] In Canada, a father objected to his underage daughter receiving cross-sex hormones. He was imprisoned for six months and fined $30,000.[38] As individual states follow Canada's lead to criminalize what it deems "conversion therapy," the U.S. may soon follow suit.

## Conclusion

I'm well aware that, to some, this chapter sounded like fearmongering, hyper-political, "culture war" stuff. An overstatement of a few extremes that misrepresents actual transgender people and their lives. Or worse, rhetoric that perpetuates harmful stereotypes that contribute to a trans person's challenges. I get that. And the last thing I intend is to dismiss genuine anxieties and concerns.

But consider: what's mainstream today was on the "fringe" not five years ago. The extremes now will soon become all too typical. I certainly can't predict the future. But if the next decade is anything like the last, we will see the extremes move to the middle of public policy and social consciousness. So, if you're a little peeved at me today but better prepared for tomorrow, I can live with that.

In our last few moments, we'll look at where we go from here and how the best way forward is the way back.

# CHAPTER 7

# Looking Back and
# Moving Forward

I magine I'm a neurologist. I've been trained to identify the symptoms of brain-based diseases and to help people obtain the treatments they need. Now imagine you come to me with symptoms that indicate something serious—like MRI, spinal-tap, CT-scan serious. But, based on conversations with friends and what you Googled online, you believe your symptoms stem from being chronically overstressed, and that if I just gave you something to help you manage this stress, you'd be fine in a few weeks.

Now, what kind of doctor would I be if, instead of ordering the tests I know you need, I simply agreed with your self-assessment and only treated your symptoms? What if I were more concerned with your temporary comfort than telling you the difficult news that your symptoms are manifestations of a bigger problem? What censure would I deserve for withholding information you need, however disappointing, even frightening, that information may be? And how would *you* feel later down the line when you discover it was a brain tumor all along, and your doctor didn't even think to scan for this risk for fear of hurting your feelings or offending your sense of what might be wrong?

If we, surrounded by such pain and confusion, neglect to represent God's design for sex and gender faithfully, we will have committed spiritual malpractice against vulnerable and hurting people. We who have been healed of soul-level diseases—who know the futility of trying and failing to treat only the symptoms—are called to proclaim the cure. Our culture prescribes confusion to discover peace. It practices mutilation to become whole.

Standing at odds with socially dominant ideas, especially ideas about sex and gender, is rarely a convenient endeavor. But, in the words of Pastor Jon Tyson, "The joy and satisfaction that come from being faithful to Christ will always be richer than the mere ease that comes from drifting along the cultural currents."[1] Difficult as it will be, we cannot afford to compromise. The cost is far too high.

## Both Unprecedented and Famliar

The Christian sexual ethic has always been antithetical to the practice of other cultures. The expectation of mutual, lifelong sexual fidelity between a man and a woman, between whom exists equal worth and dignity, was fundamentally at odds with every society it encountered. Christianity was born amid rampant sexual permissiveness.[2] The values our culture regards as traditional, even repressive, were radical to the ancient world.

As unparalleled as today's beliefs and practices are, they are nothing the people of God have not already faced. Terms and technology have changed, but human nature and the effects of our broken world have not. The desire to live as a member of the opposite gender and the feeling of disconnection from one's body go back millennia. In the time of Moses, presenting oneself as the opposite gender seems to have occurred among Israel's surrounding cultures (Duet. 22:5). The command of Deuteronomy—the Law by which God's people would know His character and be distinct from the surrounding pagan nations—indicates a connection between worshipping the Lord and acceptance of one's maleness or femaleness. First Corinthians 11, a notoriously challenging passage to interpret and apply, indicates some correlation between godliness and comporting with one's created gender. In today's vernacular, we would say God required His people to present their gender identity according to their biological sex.

Prior to modern medical and technological advancement, a person who dressed like the opposite gender was known as a transvestite, a behavior known throughout the ancient world.[3] In ancient Rome, the emperor Elagabalus (c. 204–222) was known to dress in women's clothes and preferred being called *domina* (lady) rather than *dominus* (lord).[4] He reportedly offered a fortune to any physician who could remove his genitals and give him a vagina. The cultic worship of the goddess, Cybele, involved male priests who castrated themselves and thereafter dressed as women.[5] The ancient world lacked the medical advances and philosophical beliefs of our modern age, but the impulse to divide one's gender identity from one's biological sex existed even then. Truly, there is nothing new under the sun (Eccles. 1:9).

Throughout church history, when followers of Christ encounter a culture, they defend the value of God's image bearers and protect society's most vulnerable. Saint Basil of Caesarea discovered that a guild traveled through the region providing herbal and surgical abortions, then used the aborted infant's bodies for collagen cream. He mobilized his congregation to care for abortion-vulnerable women and used his pulpit to preach against the practice. That's not all. Whether an ancient society outlawed forced prostitution was an exclusive indication of whether it had been influenced by Christianity.[6] Space prevents me from an exhaustive list, but recall Saint Patrick, who ended child sacrifice to pagan gods in Ireland;[7] Annie Armstrong, who rescued children from temple prostitution; and Lottie Moon, who opposed the torturous practice of foot binding. Today, Christians are among the most active in combating human trafficking, illiteracy, poverty, hunger, and abortion. Wherever you find the image of God being misused, harmed, and degraded, you'll find the people of God opposing injustice and defending their dignity. When Jesus called us the salt of the earth, He intended us to preserve the world from its moral decay, to slow, even counteract the process of moral decline however we can (Matt. 5:13–16).

God's ways reflect God's character. And God's character is good, true, righteous, and pure. We are His ambassadors, His servants. When we right earthly wrongs, it isn't (or at least, shouldn't be) to pursue political power or secure social preeminence, but to restrain the effects of depravity in our sinful world. Jesus didn't teach us to pray that we could overcome earthy kingdoms. He taught us to pray that His own kingdom—and by it, His righteous rule—would come to earth (Matt. 6:10). But when God's kingdom reigns through God's people, the presence of God's people will have an effect on earthly kingdoms as they seek the common good.

## Our Most Compelling Witness

Ultimately, we oppose gender ideology not because we hate humanity but precisely the opposite: because we love humanity.

Because we love God, we love what God loves—people. And for the sake of people, we speak out against ideas and practices that harm them.

Sprinkle shares the story of a man named Alan. Alan suffered from gender dysphoria and bravely shared with a Christian friend his desire to be a woman and his attraction to other men. How this friend responded was a pivotal moment in Alan's life. He expected to hear condemnation but instead heard words of mercy. Alan's friend assured him that God didn't hate him and that he was lovable to God and others. Alan gave his life to Jesus and believes that, without that word of grace, he would have transitioned to living as a woman. Commenting on this story, Sprinkle notes, "It was love, not logic, that changed Alan's heart. People are rarely argued into the kingdom."[8]

What a difference it made in one gender-confused person's life to be received with compassion and grace. To have found someone who would listen, not shame or condemn, and to be reassured of God's love. Can you imagine how different Alan's story would have been had he heard, "It's just a choice. You need to repent or leave," instead of, "Thank you for sharing that with me. Tell me what you mean by that"? To paraphrase Warren Weirsbe, love without truth is hypocrisy, but truth without love is brutality. Jesus Himself always disagreed with people in love and from love.[9] Love is patient and kind. It's never rude or arrogant. It endures the worst while believing the best. Love celebrates the truth because the truth sets us free.[10] I have no doubt gender dysphoria is a complex condition, one that requires skilled professionals to help. But what if someone's road to healing started with the same needs we all have? To belong. To be accepted. To be loved.

## Irreplacable Masterpieces

In the aftermath and recovery of World War II, Allied forces and nations pursued the recovery of great works of art. The Nazis had overwhelmed nations, invaded homes and museums, and stolen hundreds of thousands of unique and irreplaceable masterpieces. Finding them took years. Some people spent decades, even lifetimes, tracking down these priceless pieces of art. It took patience, determination, and conviction.

It might have seemed a trivial or undeserving use of time and money, especially as entire countries were rebuilding from the rubble. But these works of art were more than paintings. What these cultural treasures symbolized was more than the oil and canvas used to make them. These were emblems that depicted who people were as human beings and influenced how they related to one another.[11] They were expressions of people's identities, an identity that had been battered by the ravages of war. Their recovery was worth every ounce of effort and sacrifice.

Gender ideology has invaded and overwhelmed our social consciousness and our culture like a tyrant. It has become a cultural dictator that demands allegiance and controls through fear. And it has plundered what is immeasurably priceless—countless women (and men) created to know and reflect their Creator.

Their recovery may take decades, perhaps lifetimes. But they are worthy of our tireless effort and faithful sacrifice. We will need patience. We will need determination. And we will need the unwavering conviction that female identity symbolizes more than the physical body it comprises. Because to possess a female identity *is* to be a woman. And to be a woman is to reflect the reality and intent of the Master Artist.

# What about Intersex?

T hroughout this work, we've studied how our sexed bodies indicate and inform our gender identities. Biology
corresponds to gender.

But sometimes chromosomes and hormones get misaligned,
and an infant's reproductive anatomy is irregular. A female
infant can be born with male sex characteristics and *vice versa*.
A segment of the population is born with a Developmental Sex
Disorder (DSD), also called intersex.[1] If someone is intersex,
she is "sexually ambiguous," meaning she has a blend of the sex
characteristics of chromosomes of both sexes or she has atypical
features in her sexual anatomy. As there are more than thirty
different types of DSDs, *intersex* is an umbrella term to include
all of them.[2]

Intersex conditions can affect chromosomes, internal genitalia, external genitalia, or a combination of these. They range
from imperceptible to severe.[3] Some people live their entire lives
without realizing they have one. Others suffer significant hard-
ships, often as young children, as doctors and parents attempt to

surgically or socially conform them to one sex or the other. The phrase "sex assigned at birth" comes from how intersex infants are treated if they have an ambiguous sex (an occurrence that is, mercifully, rare).[4]

The reported percentage of intersex persons varies. Anne Fausto-Sterling claims it's as many as 1.7 percent of the population. Leonard Sax takes issue with Fausto-Sterling's statistic, saying her definition of intersex is so broad, the numbers are inflated. She included conditions in which there's little to no difficulty identifying whether someone is male or female.[5] About 88 percent of the people included in Fausto-Sterling's definition of intersex were females whose hormone levels led to irregular periods, more body hair, and a deeper voice. This isn't near the degree of sex ambiguity other intersex conditions produce.[6] Remove conditions that don't include intersex traits, and the number may be closer to 0.228 percent of the population.[7]

Whatever the statistical data finds, people aren't percentages. Preston Sprinkle observes how both ends of the political spectrum employ intersex conditions to suit their aim. Progressives magnify intersexuality and use it to argue for gender nonconformity. Conservatives tend to make the opposite error by ignoring the presence of intersex people and their struggles.[8]

## Understanding Intersex

What countless intersex people endure is heartbreaking. Many carry a stigma and a sense of shame. They have the pain of feeling out of place, marginalized, "other." Some have lived with the anguish of being medically assigned a sex before their bodies developed to indicate a dominant sexual identity.[9]

Others have had their bodies poked and prodded at tender ages. And others have undergone invasive and reconstructive surgeries before they could even consent.[10] One woman recalled emotionally excruciating examinations, begging cold and clinical doctors to stop to no avail.[11] Some have even compared it to feeling sexually abused.[12] Children are already vulnerable—how much more intersex children?

As medical science has advanced, so has the medical community's response to intersex persons. Some conditions require early surgeries since intersex anatomy can be prone to developing cancer. Others are less urgent, allowing the child to be treated in the "least invasive fashion."[13] In many intersex conditions, gender and sex identity is disordered but still identifiable; most intersex persons see themselves as a man or a woman with a birth condition like any other.[14] Today, intersex children are more likely to develop socially as a boy or girl, then have the option of surgery when they mature.[15]

## A Familiar Beginning

Though most of us will never understand the agony of being born intersex, we are all born with bodies that don't work as they should.[16] We have genetic predispositions, congenital defects, and proneness to specific cancers or conditions. We grieve over these things because our bodies matter and our bodies are good. We work to alleviate the effects of the fall because embodied human beings have intrinsic worth.

There's not a corner of our world that hasn't been broken and marred by our fallen world. Every sin, sickness, suffering, and sorrow find their start in Genesis 3. Creation itself groans under the bondage of this earthly decay (Rom. 8:22). Every day, children are tragically born with diseases, deformities, and defects. An infant born with a DSD is created in God's image. God made her body, and all that He does is good. Thus, the intersex body is good and has irrevocable dignity, not because it is perfect (none of our bodies are) but because it is created by God.[17] We can and must welcome intersex persons who are suffering from the brokenness of creation, and we should walk with them in sensitivity and love.[18] A developmental abnormality of the reproductive system should be no more a source of shame than a developmental abnormality of the limbs, the heart, or the eyes (John 9:1–3).

## Adam, Eve, and Everyone in Between

Some Christian scholars believe the presence of intersex people indicates that biological sex is not binary and that God created biological sex to be a spectrum with several variations between male and female. In her book *Sex Difference in Christian Theology*, Megan DeFranza questions whether Christianity requires a "two-sex system."[19] For DeFranza, Western culture's view of binary sex differences is "oppressive."[20] DeFranza believes we must *decenter* categories of sex, gender, and sexual identity in order to promote healing and reconciliation in the entire community of God.[21] Then we'll have the humility and love for intersex persons who have been overlooked, marginalized, and oppressed.[22]

According to DeFranza, Adam and Eve don't represent sex differences but "shared humanity." They are the *progenitors* of human beings, not *patterns*.[23] The sex differences between the first male and female were necessary to biologically begin humanity, but God's redemptive work "presses beyond" those biological categories. Thus, intersex conditions are not a result of living after the fall but part of creating a spectrum of sexual identities.

DeFranza claims intersex conditions theologically support transgender identity.[24] Insisting that Adam and Eve are examples of sex differences is an assumption we are reading into the Bible. She calls it a "false reading" that asks too much of the first few chapters of Genesis.[25] She reasons that many creations are not listed in the creation story. Genesis 1 says God created animals of the land and animals of the sea. But it doesn't mention that He made amphibians, which exist on both land and sea.[26] What about other animals that live on the spectrum of land and sea categories? Are they the result of the fall because they're not named?[27] If animals and vegetation live within a range of creation binaries, perhaps male and female do too. Perhaps the two sexes represent two extremes on a spectrum of sex differences.

But human beings aren't like the rest of God's creation. We are created in His image. Part of our embodied, image-bearing identity is a capacity for relationship that includes our bodies.[28]

## Intersex Identity = Trans Identity?

Modern gender ideology regards intersex and trans people as two equal but different minorities:[29] both disrupting the binary, both marginalized by an oppressive majority culture, and both denied the bodily autonomy they deserve.[30] If an intersex person is born with a sexual anatomy that differs from her gender identity, then the trans person can be born with a sexual anatomy that differs from her gender identity.

But this logic misses an important, and glaring, fact. Intersex conditions are biological while transgender identity is psychological. For intersex biology to validate the belief that gender identity is what really matters, we would have to ascribe greater meaning to the psychological self than to the biological self. Ironically, using intersex people to authenticate transgender claims is self-contradicting since most gender theorists insist that biology is irrelevant to gender identity.[31]

It's also worth mentioning that most people with a DSD do not identify as transgender or nonbinary. The majority of intersex persons align with the gender that corresponds to their sexual anatomy, despite being born with an irregularity.[32]

Notwithstanding the variations among intersex people, there are still two sexes. Intersex conditions are combinations of, or deviations from, the binary of male or female.[33] But there is no third sex or third set of hormones. There isn't even a third reproductive anatomy that combines male and female reproductive anatomy. Instead, DSDs are a blending of both male and female.

Intersex persons are human beings created in God's image. They are precious people who are worthy of dignity and respect. They were created for relationship. And they happen to have been born with a blend of the two biological sexes.[34] Of all the communities who can understand the effects of a fallen world and see past those effects to one's full humanity, it's the body of Christ.

# APPENDIX B

# Is Gender Dysphoria Brain Based?

In the last decade, neurologists have searched for a brain-based or genetic cause of gender dysphoria. It's a daunting task: human beings have tens of thousands of genes, and even minor traits are polygenetic, meaning they come from multiple genetic codes.[1] But identifying a genetic or neurological cause of gender nonconformity may prove that sex and gender aren't binary after all.

One study looked at hormonal differences by analyzing cellular proteins called hormone receptors. Hormone receptors tell our hormones what to do; they're like the supervisors of estrogen (female) and androgen (male). A 2005 Swedish study analyzed estrogen receptor genes in male-to-female (MtF) transsexuals, looking for DNA changes that might influence gender. It found certain repeated sequences in MtF transsexuals that were different from nontranssexuals.[2] But the researchers also issued a warning. They said interpreting their findings required "utmost caution." They also acknowledged that the gene variants they studied were "relatively common," and none of them could be considered a "primary cause" of transsexualism.[3]

Another study claimed to discover a brain-based link between neurobiology and homosexuality. The research is from 1991, but scientists draw on its findings to research transgender identity. It examined a cluster of cells in the hypothalamus, the part of the brain that manages hormones, and measured its size.[4] Researchers found that, among those of homosexual men, this cluster of cells was closer in size to heterosexual women than it was to heterosexual men. The study's author was cautious about the results and said they were speculative. The research didn't determine whether this pattern was a *cause* or a *consequence* of homosexuality.[5] Additionally, the experiment was conducted again and failed to produce the same results.[6] Thus, the research was inconclusive.[7]

In 2018, researchers claimed to have found a neurological basis between gender dysphoria and adolescents.[8] They also studied the hypothalamus, but this time they compared how it behaved differently among boys and girls who had gender dysphoria. It stated that gender-dysphoric adolescents had a hypothalamus that acted more like their "experienced gender" than their natal sex. In other words, a biological female who identified as a boy had a hypothalamus that responded more like a male than a female.[9] But dig a little deeper, and you'll find the results aren't quite so cut-and-dried. Dr. Michelle Cretella is the former president of the American Pediatric Society. She claims a single MRI scan of a person's hypothalamus isn't enough to determine transgender identity or establish its cause. Dr. Martin Bednar, a neurosurgeon and neuroscientist, elaborated, saying a single MRI scan only shows what is happening at a moment in time.

It doesn't demonstrate patterns over a period of time. It would take multiple MRIs to determine whether the study's conclusion reflects biological differences that are "inherent and immutable" or if it simply shows "a consequence of brain plasticity."[10]

The results of these studies vary, and they haven't been repeated to produce consistent results. Thus far, medical research has not identified a neurological or a genetic cause that determines gender or gender identity. In one way or another, they have come up short.[11] In 2020, a group of scientists reviewed all the relevant research on the biological basis of sexual development, specifically focusing on the impact of sex hormones and genetic background on the development of sex difference and gender identity."[12] They concluded that researchers have yet to identify a convincing genetic candidate.

## Causes, Correlations, and Contradictions

But what if there were? What if, a few years from now, neuroscientists find irrefutable evidence of a brain-based link between biology and gender dysphoria? Would the binary be broken? It might, apart from one important factor.

Correlation does not equal causation.[13] People who have gender dysphoria may have a common neurological trait, one that corresponds to their gender identity. But whether that trait is the *cause* of their gender identity is a different question. Moreover, while our biology *influences* behavior, it doesn't *control* behavior, a theory known as biological determinism.[14]

As significant as genetics are, they cannot exclusively account for how the brain functions. Within the framework of our biology, our brains are "plastic," meaning they are capable of change. The brain's "neuroplasticity" means it can create and strengthen new neural pathways as well as eliminate other neural pathways, a process called "synaptic pruning."[15] For instance, a stroke survivor can relearn how to walk and talk because his brain moves information away from the damaged area and into an undamaged area. When the brain receives and reinforces information, its structure changes.

This isn't just at the level of what you think but also what you do. Every choice you make strengthens the neural pathways in your brain. In the words of one brain researcher, "The primary driver of change in your brain is your behavior."[16] Learning how to navigate your upgraded iPhone, remembering how to drive to a new coffee shop, and figuring out how to play the guitar all create structural changes in your brain. These changes occur rapidly and dramatically.[17] The same principle applies to ideas and beliefs. A clinic in Colorado helps patients overcome paralysis using a method called Neuroplastic Functional Training.[18] It found that patients who received a prognosis of lifelong paralysis neurologically adapted to that belief. The structure of their brains was hindered from relearning and regaining certain functions. Before patients could walk again, they had to accept the belief that they *could* walk again. As a result, the brain adapted to the "new information" and eventually created new neural pathways around the damaged ones.

What does this have to do with gender identity? Neuroplasticity, or the brain's ability to adapt to environmental stimuli, makes it nearly impossible to establish a cause-and-effect relationship between the human brain and gender identity. Our bodies, brains, beliefs, and behaviors are deeply interconnected and not easily untangled.

Even if scientists identified a neurological basis for transgender identity, they would also have to prove the pattern demonstrated a cause and not just a correlation. Essentially, they would have to rule out the effect of neuroplasticity. In Dr. Cretella's estimation, "[A]ll trans brain studies to date . . . fail to disprove what is most probable: *believing one is trans and behaving trans changes the individual's brain appearance and function.*"[19] Those who claim science has discovered a neurological basis for gender dysphoria are overstating the outcomes and, at times, misrepresenting the data.

Ironically, in light of modern gender theory, it's curious these studies even exist. If gender identity is a purely subjective experience—one that is unrelated to the human body—why does it matter if it has a biological basis? Whether it starts in the brain, the genes, or the chromosomes would be irrelevant and self-refuting. Why search for evidence that biology *corresponds* to gender identity in order to justify the belief that biology *does not correspond* to gender identity? Perhaps, despite cultural assertions, we instinctively look to ground reality in empirical facts. And perhaps, too, we know deep down that there is meaning to be found in the human body, that our inner selves are inextricably tied to it, no matter how much our culture attempts to divide them.

# Glossary

**AFAB:** Assigned Female at Birth.

**Agender:** Someone who identifies as neither a man nor a woman.

**Ally:** A person who defends, supports, and promotes gender minorities; someone who does not necessarily represent a gender minority but leverages his or her social privilege and power to publicly advocate for the LQBTQIA+ community.

**AMAB:** Assigned Male at Birth.

**Asexual:** Someone who does not experience sexual attraction to others.

**Bigender:** Someone with two gender identities.

**Biological Sex:** The chromosomal, physical, and reproductive traits that indicate maleness or femaleness.

**Cisgender:** A person whose gender identity and gender expression correspond with his or her biological sex; derived from the Latin word meaning "on the same side."

**Demigender:** Feeling a partial connection to a gender identity.

**Developmental Sex Disorder (DSD):** A chromosomal, genetic, or reproductive condition that may affect the appearance and/or function of one's sexual anatomy.

**Female-to-Male (FtM):** A female-to-male transgender person.

**Gender:** The behavioral, cultural, or psychological traits typically associated with or appropriate to biological sex, which identifies a person as a man or a woman.[1]

**Gender Dysphoria:** A psychological condition in which one's gender identity does not align with one's biological sex, often causing acute mental distress; the desire to be a different gender than that which corresponds to one's biology. Degrees of gender dysphoria can range from mild to severe.

**Gender Expression:** How one manifests or expresses one's gender identity, including clothing, mannerisms, name, pronouns, etc.

**Gender Fluidity:** The change over time that someone experiences in gender identity and/or gender expression; reflects how one's gender identity can be different in different situations.

**Gender Identity:** A person's internal experience or sense of gender.

**Intersex:** A genetic or chromosomal condition that describes the range of developmental sex disorders.

**LGBTQIA+:** Lesbian, Gay, Bisexual, Transgender, Questioning/Queer, Intersex, and Asexual. The "+" maintains space for additional or emerging gender identities.

**LGBTQQIP2SAA:** Lesbian, Gay, Bisexual, Transgender, Queer, Questioning, Intersex, Pansexual, Two-Spirit, Asexual, and Ally.

**Male-to-Female (MtF):** A male-to-female transgender person.

**Nonbinary:** Someone who does not exclusively identify with one gender or the other.

**Pangender:** Someone with multiple gender identities that shift over time.

**Pansexual:** Someone who is sexually attracted to any gender.

**Pass/Passing:** To present as a gender identity convincingly or to be perceived as a certain gender identity by others.

**Present As:** To express oneself according to a certain gender identity.

**Transgender:** A person who identifies as someone of a different gender than that which corresponds to his or her biological sex.

**Transition:** A process or event of changing one's presentation of gender or physical characteristics to align with one's gender identity.

**Transsexual:** Formerly used more frequently to refer to transgender persons; often used to describe someone who has undergone medical gender transition.

**SAAB:** Sex Assigned At Birth.

**Xenogender:** A gender that cannot be understood in exclusively human terms; may incorporate the identity of plants, animals, or other creatures.

# Recommended Reading

Anderson, Ryan T. *When Harry Became Sally: Responding to the Transgender Movement*. New York: Encounter Books, 2018.

Comer, John Mark. *Live No Lies: Recognize and Resist the Three Enemies That Sabotage Your Peace*. Colorado Springs: WaterBrook, 2021.

Favale, Abigail. *The Genesis of Gender: A Christian Theory*. San Francisco: Ignatius Press, 2022.

Pearcey, Nancy. *Love Thy Body: Answering Hard Question about Life and Sexuality*. Grand Rapids, MI: Baker Books, 2018.

Shreir, Abigail. *Irreversible Damage: The Transgender Craze Seducing Our Daughters*. Washington, DC: Regnery Publishing, 2020.

Sprinkle, Preston. *Embodied: Transgender Identities, the Church, and What the Bible Has to Say*. Colorado Springs: David C. Cook, 2021.

Trueman, Carl. *Strange New World: How Thinkers and Activists Redefined Identity and Sparked the Sexual Revolution.* Wheaton, IL: Crossway, 2022.

Walker, Andrew T. *God and the Transgender Debate: What Does the Bible Actually Say about Gender Identity?*, expanded and updated. Epsom, Surrey, UK: The Good Book Company, 2022.

# Notes

## Introduction: Cultural Chaos and Contagious Confusion

1. Abigail Favale, *The Genesis of Gender: A Christian Theory* (San Francisco: Ignatius Press, 2022), 169.

2. Abigail Shreir, *Irreversible Damage: The Transgender Craze Seducing Our Daughters* (Washington, DC: Regnery Publishing, 2020), xxvii, 32.

3. Jake Thibault, *Transgender Ideology & Gender Dysphoria: A Catholic Response* (Providence, RI: Maryvale Press, 2021), 464.

4. Favale, *Genesis of Gender*, 147.

5. "The Controversy over Trans Teens," *The Week*, October 24, 2021, https://theweek.com/life/1006253/the-controversy-over-trans-teens.

6. Jason Rafferty, "Gender Identity Development in Children," HealthyChildren.org, last updated May 11, 2022, https://www.healthychildren.org/English/agesstages/gradeschool/Pages/Gender-Identity-and-Gender-Confusion-In-Children.aspx.

7. @LibsofTikTok, *Twitter*, August 13, 2022, https://twitter.com/libsoftiktok/status/1558669742126223361.

8. @BillboardChris, Twitter, August 29, 2022, https://twitter.com/BillboardChris/status/1564330483588251650.

9. Andy Rose, "Vanderbilt Transgender Health Clinic Suspends Gender-Affirming Surgery for Minors," CNN, October 9, 2022, https://www.cnn.com/2022/10/09/us/vanderbilt-suspends

-gender-affirming-surgery-minors/index.html. @MattWalshBlog, *Twitter*, September 20, 2022, https://twitter.com/MattWalshBlog /status/1572313523232931840?s=20&t=JoP3phnGWfblz6ZBwVTJzg.

10. Helen Joyce, *Trans: When Ideology Meets Reality* (London: Oneworld Publications, 2021), 83.

11. Joyce, *Trans*, 94.

12. Russell Goldman, "Here's a List of 58 Gender Options for Facebook Users," ABC News, February 13, 2014, https://abcnews.go .com/blogs/headlines/2014/02/heres-a-list-of-58-gender-options-for -facebook-users.

13. Shaziya Allarakha, "What Are the 72 Other Genders?" MedicineNet, February 2, 2022, https://www.medicinenet.com /what_are_the_72_other_genders/article.htm.

14. "Blankgirl," LGBTA+Wiki, https://www.lgbtqia.wiki/wiki /Blankgirl.

15. "Xenogender," Gender Wiki, accessed November 18, 2022, https://gender.fandom.com/wiki/Xenogender.

16. "Your Line of Questioning Is Transphobic," C-Span, YouTube, July 12, 2022, https://www.youtube.com/watch?v=Fed5RzXyU20.

17. Marisa Iati, "Booksellers Association Apologizes for 'Violent' Distribution of 'Anti-Trans' Title," *Washington Post*, July 16, 2021, https://www.washingtonpost.com/lifestyle/2021/07/16/irreversible -damage-anti-trans-booksellers-association.

18. Katie McCoy, "FIRST PERSON: Gender Ideology and the Silencing of Dissent," Baptist Press, February 9, 2022, https://www .baptistpress.com/resource-library/news/first-person-gender-ideology -and-the-silencing-of-dissent. Several conservative writers and scholars have faced campaigns for their professional dismissal and been removed from social media platforms for expressing their beliefs about gender.

19. Preston Sprinkle, *Embodied: Transgender Identities, the Church, and What the Bible Has to Say* (Colorado Springs: David C. Cook, 2021), 152.

20. Jillian McKoy, "US Suicide Rates Are Stagnant or Rising among Many Groups, Despite Overall National Decline," Boston University School of Public Health, April 14, 2022, https://www.bu

.edu/sph/news/articles/2022/us-suicides-are-stagnant-or-on-the-rise
-among-many-groups.

21. Sprinkle, *Embodied*, 31.

22. "X Dysphoria," TransHub, accessed November 5, 2022,
https://www.transhub.org.au/dysphoria.

## Chapter 1: How: The Formative Effect of Social Influence

1. Rikki Schlott, "'I Literally Lost Organs:' Why Detransitioned
Teens Regret Changing Genders," *New York Post*, June 18, 2022,
https://nypost.com/2022/06/18/detransitioned-teens-explain-why
-they-regret-changing-genders.

2. The condition was also rare, representing about .01 percent
of the population, or one in ten thousand births. See "Intersex"
Appendix.

3. Jake Thibault, *Transgender Ideology and Gender Dysphoria: A
Catholic Response* (Providence, RI: Maryville Catholic Press, 2021),
463.

4. Lisa Littman, "Parent Reports of Adolescents and Young
Adults Perceived to Show Signs of a Rapid Onset of Gender
Dysphoria," PLOS One, 13, no. 8 (August 16, 2018); 13, https://
journals.plos.org/plosone/article/file?id=10.1371/journal.pone
.0202330&type=printable.

5. Littman, "Parent Reports of Adolescents and Young Adults,"
12. "Most (86.7%) of the parents reported that, along with the
sudden or rapid onset of gender dysphoria, their child either had
an increase in their social media/internet use, belonged to a
friend group in which one or multiple friends became transgender-
identified during a similar time frame, or both."

6. "Social Contagion," American Psychological Association,
accessed November 18, 2022, https://dictionary.apa.org/social-
contagion.

7. See Chapter 4.

8. Jordan Peterson, season 4, episode 11: Abigail Shrier, podcast, 2022.

9. Thibault, *Transgender Ideology and Gender Dysphoria*, 464.

10. "Am I Trans?," *The Gender Dysphoria Bible*, accessed November 18, 2022, https://genderdysphoria.fyi/en/am-i-trans.

11. Abigail Shrier, *Irreversible Damage: The Transgender Craze Seducing Our Daughters* (Washington, DC: Regnery Publishing, 2020), 154.

12. Littman, "Parent Reports of Adolescents and Young Adults," 20.

13. Schlott, "'I Literally Lost Organs': Why Detransitioned Teens Regret Changing Genders."

14. Shrier, *Irreversible Damage*, 136–37.

15. Abigail Favale, *The Genesis of Gender: A Christian Theory* (San Francisco: Ignatius Press, 2022), 148.

16. Shrier, *Irreversible Damage*, 140.

17. Shrier, *Irreversible Damage*, 39; Littman, "Parent Reports of Adolescents and Young Adults," 2, 34.

18. Shrier, *Irreversible Damage*, 97–98.

19. Shrier, *Irreversible Damage*, 97, 105.

20. Shrier, *Irreversible Damage*, 102.

21. Sand C. Chang, Anneliese Singh, Lore M. Dickey, *A Clinician's Guide to Gender Affirming Care: Working with Transgender and Gender Nonconforming Clients* (Oakland, CA: Context Press, 2018). 1.

22. Chang, et al., *A Clinician's Guide to Gender Affirming Care*, 2.

23. Shrier, *Irreversible Damage*, 101. The answer is none. Yet.

24. "AAP Policy Statement Urges Support and Care of Transgender and Gender-Diverse Children and Adolescents," HealthyChildren.org, September 17, 2018, https://www.healthychildren.org/English/news/Pages/Support-for-Transgender-and-Gender-Diverse-Children-and-Adolescents.aspx.

25. Colt Keo-Meier and Diane Ehrensaft, "Introduction to the Gender Affirmative Model," in *The Gender Affirming Model: An Interdisciplinary Approach to Supporting Transgender and Gender Expansive Children* (Washington, DC: American Psychological Association, 2018), 5. Rebecca A. Clay, "Embracing a Gender-Affirming Model for Transgender Youth," *American Psychological*

*Association,* 49, no. 8 (2018), https://www.apa.org/monitor/2018/09/ce-corner.

26. American Psychological Association, "Guidelines for Psychological Practice with Transgender and Gender Nonconforming People," accessed November 18, 2022, *America Psychologist,* 70, no. 9 (2015): 835.

27. The World Professional Association for Transgender Health, *Standards of Care for the Health of Transsexual, Transgender, and Gender Nonconforming People,* https://www.wpath.org/media/cms/Documents/SOC%20v7/SOC%20V7_English.pdf.

28. According to gender-affirming therapist Randi Kaufman, detransitioning is rare. She claims, "By adolescence, most adolescents have a pretty good sense of how to discern their differences between things like gender identity, gender role, and gender expression, which is how you express your gender with your dress, your hair, your mannerism, your names, your pronouns, things like that. . . . It's pretty rare by adolescence for people to change their mind." Shrier, *Irreversible Damage,* 104. Kaufman's claim fails to reflect the detransitioner community.

29. Shrier, *Irreversible Damage,* 108.

30. Shrier, *Irreversible Damage,* 123.

31. Brynn Tannehill, "The End of the Desistence Myth," *Huffington Post,* January 1, 2016, https://www.huffpost.com/entry/the-end-of-the-desistance_b_8903690.

32. Julian Vigo, "The Myth of the 'Desistence Myth,'" *Public Discourse,* July 2, 2018, https://www.thepublicdiscourse.com/2018/07/21972.

33. Ryan T. Anderson, *When Harry Became Sally: Responding to the Transgender Movement* (New York: Encounter Books, 2018), 123–25. Shrier, *Irreversible Damage,* 124.

34. Anderson, *When Harry Became Sally,* 123–25.

35. Anderson, *When Harry Became Sally,* 125: "Any intervention that interferes with the likelihood of resolution is unwarranted and potential harmful," says Dr. Paul Hruz.

36. Jesse Singal, "How the Fight Over Transgender Kids Got a Leading Sex Researcher Fired," *The Cut,* February 7, 2016, https://

www.thecut.com/2016/02/fight-over-trans-kids-got-a-researcher
-fired.html.

37. Anderson, *When Harry Became Sally*, 120.

38. Grace Lidinsky-Smith, "There's No Standard for Care When It Comes to Trans Medicine," *Newsweek*, June 25, 2021, https://www.newsweek.com/theres-no-standard-care-when-it-comes
-trans-medicine-opinion-1603450.

39. Anderson, *When Harry Became Sally*, 136, 140.

40. Anderson, *When Harry Became Sally*, 139. Laura Perry, *Transgender to Transformed: A Story of Transition That Will Truly Set You Free* (Bartlesville, OK: Genesis Publishing Group, 2019).

41. Anderson, *When Harry Became Sally*, 137. Both have what Dr. Zucker describes as a "predisposition for obsessional or focused interests and extreme rigidity and thinking." This can also be accompanied by "intense anxiety" in response to any interference with the obsession. One boy with autism fixated on gender identity for a season then fixated on a different interest. Simon Baron-Cohen explores this correlation in his work *The Essential Difference: The Truth about the Male and Female Brain* (New York: Basic Books, 2003). Baron-Cohen classifies autism as an "extreme male brain" in its capacity for systematizing.

42. Victoria G., "I Took My Teen to a Gender Clinic. This Is What Happened," *Foundation Against Intolerance & Racism*, June 20, 2022, https://fairforall.substack.com/p/gender-clinic.

43. Thibault, *Transgender Ideology and Gender Dysphoria*, 465.

44. Some children "latch onto gender dysphoria as a way of coping with trauma or other distress," Shrier, *Irreversible Damage*, 123. See also Littman, "Parent Reports of Adolescents and Young Adults."

45. Erin Brewer and Maria Keffler, "Introduction" and "Gender Dysphoria," *Transing Our Children* (Arlington, VA: Advocates Protecting Children, 2021).

46. Erin Brewer and Maria Keffler, *Always Erin* (Arlington, VA: Advocates Protecting Children, 2021).

47. "Erin Brewer: I'm Going to Be a Boy, I'll Be Safe," Ruth Institute, accessed November 18, 2022, https://ruthinstitute.org/dr-j-show/i-am-going-to-be-a-boy-it-will-keep-me-safe.

48. Littman, "Parent Reports of Adolescents and Young Adults," 36.

49. Shrier, *Irreversible Damage*, 107.

50. Marcus Evans, "Why I Resigned from Tavistock: Trans-Identified Children Need Therapy, Not Just 'Affirmation' and Drugs," *Quilette*, January 17, 2020, https://quillette.com/2020/01/17/why-i-resigned-from-tavistock-trans-identified-children-need-therapy-not-just-affirmation-and-drugs.

51. Jeremiah Keenan, "'Doctor' Advises Threatening Suicide to Get Transgender Treatments for Kids," *The Federalist*, April 1, 2019, https://thefederalist.com/2019/04/01/doctor-advises-threatening-suicide-get-transgender-treatments-kids.

52. Rikki Schlott, "'I Literally Lost Organs:' Why Detransitioned Teens Regret Changing Genders," *New York Post*, June 18, 2022; https://nypost.com/2022/06/18/detransitioned-teens-explain-why-they-regret-changing-genders. "Although medical intervention for minors requires parental consent, many mothers and fathers approve surgery and hormone therapy at the recommendation of affirming medical professionals or even out of *fear* their child might self-harm if denied treatment."

53. Ann P. Haas and Phillip L. Rodgers, "Suicide Attempts among Transgender and Gender Non-Conforming Adults," American Foundation for Suicide Prevention, January 2014, https://williamsinstitute.law.ucla.edu/wp-content/uploads/Trans-GNC-Suicide-Attempts-Jan-2014.pdf. Contrast this with .5 percent of the general population and between 10 and 20 percent of the lesbian, gay, and bisexual community.

54. "The 41% Trans Suicide Attempt Rate: A Tale of Flawed Data and Lazy Journalists," *4th Wave Now*, August 3, 2015, https://4thwavenow.com/2015/08/03/the-41-trans-suicide-rate-a-tale-of-flawed-data-and-lazy-journalists; Jane W. Robbins and Vernadette R. Broyles, "The Myth about Suicide and Gender Dysphoric Children," American College of Pediatricians study, https://acpeds

.org/assets/for-GID-page-1-The-Myth-About-Suicide-and-Gender
-Dysphoric-Children-handout.pdf.

55. Anderson, *When Harry Became Sally*, 103.

56. Jane W. Robbins and Vernadette R. Broyles, "The Myth about Suicide and Gender Dysphoric Children," American College of Pediatricians study, https://acpeds.org/assets/for-GID-page-1-The -Myth-About-Suicide-and-Gender-Dysphoric-Children-handout .pdf.

57. Robbins and Broyles, "The Myth about Suicide and Gender Dysphoric Children."

58. Robbins and Broyles, "The Myth about Suicide and Gender Dysphoric Children." "Suicide risk among trans-identified youth is less than or comparable to that of other at-risk groups of youths. Being trans-identified increases suicide risk by a factor of 13. Anorexia increases risk by a factor of 18–31. Depression multiplies it by a factor of 20. Autism raises the risk by a factor of 8. A 2019 study confirms the findings of sixteen studies dated 1969–2012, all showing that psychotherapy can be highly effective in treating underlying causes of gender incongruence such that trans identifying patients embrace their biological sex." Another doctor describes the scientific literature supporting transgender treatments as the "lowest form of scientific evidence; small studies, with few patients, followed for short periods, all of them biased by self-selection."

59. Shrier, *Irreversible Damage*, 127.

60. *The Week Staff*, "What the Tavistock Clinic's Closure Means for the Trans Debate," *The Week*, August 2, 2022, https://www .theweek.co.uk/news/science-health/957525/tavistock-clinic-closure -trans-rights-debate; https://www.thetimes.co.uk/article/tavistock -child-gender-clinic-forced-to-close-over-safety-fears-2gfj325lt.

61. Dan Ladden-Hall, "Britain Shuts Down Its Only Gender Clinic for Kids after Furious Debate," *The Blaze*, July 28, 2022, https://www.thedailybeast.com/britain-shuts-down-the-tavistock-its -only-gender-identity-clinic-for-kids-after-furious-debate.

62. Shrier, *Irreversible Damage*, 118.

63. Jamie Doward, "Governor of Tavistock Foundation Quits over Damning Report into Gender Identity Clinic," *The Guardian*,

February 23, 2019, https://www.theguardian.com/society/2019/feb
/23/child-transgender-service-governor-quits-chaos; Marcus Evans,
"Vulnerable Youngsters Rushed into Treatment. Staff Too Nervous
to Speak Out: After Resigning from Controversial Tavistock
Gender Clinic Trust, a Former Governor Says He Fears We're
Hurrying Children Down a Transgender Path They May Bitterly
Regret," DailyMail, March 1, 2019, https://www.dailymail.co.uk
/news/article-6762379/Former-governor-says-fears-hurrying-children
-transgender-path.html.

64. Shrier, *Irreversible Damage*, 117. Broader data bear this out:
96 percent of adolescents who attempted suicide had at least one
mental illness, one that could be treated with medication and psychotherapy. See American College of Pediatricians study.

65. Shrier, *Irreversible Damage*, 138.

66. "Best Practices and Recommendations for Reporting on
Suicide," Reporting on Suicide, https://reportingonsuicide.org/wp
-content/uploads/2022/05/ROS-001-One-Pager-1.13.pdf.

67. Robbins and Broyles, "The Myth about Suicide and Gender
Dysphoric Children."

68. Anderson, *When Harry Became Sally*, 97.

## Chapter 2: Why: The Ideas That Dominate Our Sense of Self

1. Carl Trueman, *Strange New World: How Thinkers and Activists
Redefined Identity and Sparked the Sexual Revolution* (Wheaton, IL:
Crossway, 2022). Carl Trueman, *The Rise and Triumph of the Modern
Self: Cultural Amnesia, Expressive Individualism, and the Road to
Sexual Revolution* (Wheaton, IL: Crossway, 2020).

2. Andrew T. Walker, *God and the Transgender Debate: What
Does the Bible Actually Say about Gender Identity?*, expanded and
updated (Epsom, Surrey, UK: The Good Book Company, 2022),
16–17.

3. John Mark Comer, *Live No Lies: Recognize and Resist
the Three Enemies That Sabotage Your Peace* (Colorado Springs:
WaterBrook, 2021).

4. Mark Sayers, *Disappearing Church: From Cultural Relevance
to Gospel Resilience* (Chicago: Moody Publishers, 2016), 15–16.

5. Abigail Favale, *The Genesis of Gender: A Christian Theory* (San Francisco: Ignatius Press, 2022), 18.

6. Favale, *The Genesis of Gender*, 18.

7. Walker, *God and the Transgender Debate*, 15.

8. Walker, *God and the Transgender Debate*, 14–15.

9. Walker, *God and the Transgender Debate*, 20.

10. Trueman, *Strange New World*, 21–22.

11. Trevin Wax, "Expressive Individualism: What Is It?," The Gospel Coalition, October 16, 2018, https://www.thegospelcoalition.org/blogs/trevin-wax/expressive-individualism-what-is-it.

12. Trueman, *Strange New World*, 23.

13. Trueman, *Strange New World*, 22.

14. Trueman, *Strange New World*, 23; Charles Taylor, *Sources of the Self: The Making of Modern Identity* (Cambridge: Harvard University Press, 1989), 475.

15. Trueman, *Strange New World*, 22.

16. Wax, "Expressive Individualism: What Is It?"

17. Wax, "Expressive Individualism: What Is It?"

18. Walker, *God and the Transgender Debate*, 17.

19. Trueman, *Strange New World*, 31.

20. Trueman, *Strange New World*, 141.

21. Trueman, *Strange New World*, 35.

22. Trueman, *Strange New World*, 37–38, 40–41.

23. Trueman, *Strange New World*, 41.

24. Trueman, *Strange New World*, 47.

25. Trueman, *Strange New World*, 62.

26. Trueman, *Strange New World*, 64.

27. Trueman, *Strange New World*, 63.

28. Trueman, *Strange New World*, 59.

29. Phil Gasper, "Marxism, Morality, and Human Nature," *International Socialist Review*, issue 82, https://isreview.org/issue/82/marxism-morality-and-human-nature/index.html.

30. Trueman, *Strange New World*, 55–58.

31. Diana H. Coole, *Women in Political Theory: From Ancient Misogyny to Contemporary Feminism* (Sussex, UK: Wheatsheaf Books, 1988), 187.

32. Both Marx and Friedrich Engels believed the communist revolution would bring a decrease in the difference between man and woman. It was key to true equality in the world. Trueman, *Strange New World*, 132.

33. Friedrich Engels, *The Origin of the Family, Private Property and the State* (London: Electric Book Company Ltd, 2001), 92. For Engels, liberating marriage from economic constraints would almost redeem it. People would be free to choose a partner without the consideration of economic security. "Full freedom of marriage can become generally operative only when the abolition of capitalist production, and the property relations created by it, has removed all those secondary economic considerations which still exert so powerful an influence on the choice of a partner. Then, no other motive remains than mutual inclination" (98).

34. Jarrett Stepman, "I Went to a Socialism Conference. Here are 6 Shocking Things I Learned," *The National Interest*, July 15, 2019, https://nationalinterest.org/blog/buzz/i-went-socialism -conference-here-are-6-shocking-things-i-learned-67057.

35. John Mark Comer, "Live No Lies Podcast: Episode 4 with Dr. Nancy Pearcey," YouTube, October 6, 2021, https://www.youtube .com/watch?v=FPMi7uquliw.

36. Trueman, *Strange New World*, 82.

37. Walker, *God and the Transgender Debate*, 18.

38. "The Sexual Revolution Created Identity Politics—Mary Eberstadt," TRIGGERnometry podcast, May 2, 2021, https://pod casts.apple.com/au/podcast/sexual-revolution-created-identity-poli tics-mary-eberstadt/id1375568988?i=1000519743563.

39. Robert Bork, *Slouching towards Gomorrah: Modern Liberalism and American Decline* (New York: Regan Books, 2010).

40. "The Sexual Revolution Created Identity Politics—Mary Eberstadt."

41. See glossary.

42. Trueman, *Strange New World*, 25.

43. Trueman, *Strange New World*, 25.

44. Trueman, *Strange New World*, 71–74.

45. Trueman, *Rise and Triumph of the Modern Self*, 222.

46. Trueman, *Rise and Triumph of the Modern Self*, 221, 266.

47. Trueman, *Strange New World*, 75.

48. Nancy Pearcey, *Total Truth: Liberating Christianity from Its Cultural Captivity* (Wheaton, IL: Crossway, 2008), 145.

49. Pearcey, *Total Truth*, 144.

50. *Masters of Sex*, created by Michele Ashford, Showtime, 2013–2016. *Kinsey*, directed by Bill Condon, Fox Searchlight Pictures, 2004.

51. Robert H. Knight, "How Alfred C. Kinsey's Sex Studies Have Harmed Women and Children," Concerned Women for America, https://concernedwomen.org/images/content/kinsey -women_11_03.pdf.

52. Trueman, *Strange New World*, 25.

53. Carl R. Trueman, "Should Our Sexual Desires Determine Who We Really Are?," Crossway, March 24, 2022, https://www.crossway .org/articles/should-our-sexual-desires-determine-who-we-really-are.

54. Trueman, *Strange New World*, 88.

55. Trueman, *Strange New World*, 80.

56. Christopher Turner, "Wilhelm Reich: The Man Who Invented Free Love," *The Guardian*, July 8, 2011, https://www .theguardian.com/books/2011/jul/08/wilhelm-reich-free-love -orgasmatron.

57. Trueman, *Strange New World*, 87.

58. Trueman, *Rise and Triumph of the Modern Self*, 235.

59. Trueman, *Rise and Triumph of the Modern Self*, 233.

60. Trueman, *Rise and Triumph of the Modern Self*, 235.

61. Trueman, *Rise and Triumph of the Modern Self*, 235.

62. Trueman, *Rise and Triumph of the Modern Self*, 236.

63. Trueman, *Strange New World*, 83.

64. Trueman, *Rise and Triumph of the Modern Self*, 237.

65. Trueman, *Rise and Triumph of the Modern Self*, 237.

66. Lil Miss Hot Mess, "Drag Queens Won't Be Cowed by Haters. The Story Goes On," NBC News, June 20, 2022, https:// www.nbcnews.com/think/opinion/drag-queens-story-hour-goes-on -rcna34169.

67. Debra Soh, *The End of Gender: Debunking the Myths about Sex and Identity in Our Society* (New York: Threshold Editions, 2020), 19.

## Chapter 3: Where: The Relational Sphere and Validation of Gender Identity

1. "How to Simulate a Period (for Transgender Women)," YouTube, September 1, 2015, https://www.youtube.com/watch?v =BcNco-mM700.

2. David McFadden, "Fertility Frontier: Can Transgender Women Get Uterus Transplants?," McGill, March 19, 2021, https://www.mcgill.ca/channels/channels/news/fertility-frontier-can -transgender-women-get-uterus-transplants-329760; Leah Samuel, "With Womb Transplants a Reality, Transgender Women Dare to Dream of Pregnancies," STAT, March 7, 2016, https://www.statnews .com/2016/03/07/uterine-transplant-transgender.

3. Alex Oliveira, "Furious Florida Mother Sues 13-Year-Old Daughter's School after Teachers Created a 'Transgender Support Plan' WITHOUT Her Consent because the Girl Questioned Her Gender When Friends Started Identifying as Trans," *Daily Mail*, May 2, 2022, https://www.dailymail.co.uk/news/article-10775329 /Mother-sues-school-helps-daughter-transition-without-parental -consent.html; Donna St. George, "Gender Transitions at School Spur Debate over When, or if, Parents Are Told," *Washington Post*, July 18, 2022, https://www.washingtonpost.com/education/2022/07 /18/gender-transition-school-parent-notification.

4. Lane Moore, "A Complete Beginner's Guide to Chest Binding," *Cosmopolitan*, March 21, 2016, https://www.cosmopolitan .com/sex-love/news/a55546/how-to-bind-your-chest.

5. Breast binding has been linked to damaged breast tissue.

6. Ryan Anderson, *When Harry Became Sally* (New York: Encounter Books, 2018), 124.

7. Anderson, *When Harry Became Sally*, 125. Because of this, Dr. Zucker expects the desistence rate to drop.

8. Abigail Shrier, *Irreversible Damage: The Transgender Craze Seducing Our Daughters* (Washington, DC: Regnery Publishing, 2020), 112.

9. "Endocrine Society Urges Policymakers to Follow Science on Transgender Health," Endocrine Society, October 28, 2019, https://www.endocrine.org/news-and-advocacy/news-room/2019/transgender-custody-statement#:~:text=Suppressing%20puberty%20is%20fully%20reversible,this%20population%20improves%20psychological%20functioning.

10. "Puberty Blockers," St. Louis Children's Hospital, https://www.stlouischildrens.org/conditions-treatments/transgender-center/puberty-blockers.

11. "Puberty Blockers."

12. Lisa Littman, "Parent Reports of Adolescents and Young Adults Perceived to Show Signs of a Rapid Onset of Gender Dysphoria," PLOS One, 13, no. 8 (August 16, 2018): 25, https://journals.plos.org/plosone/article/file?id=10.1371/journal.pone.0202330&type=printable.

13. Jake Thibault, *Transgender Ideology & Gender Dysphoria: A Catholic Response* (Providence, RI: Maryville Catholic Press, 2021), 485.

14. Anderson, *When Harry Became Sally*, 130. "FDA Warns of Brain Swelling and Permanent Vision Loss Found in Children Taking Puberty Blockers," Sex Change Regret, July 25, 2022, https://sexchangeregret.com/fda-warns-of-brain-swelling-and-permanent-vision-loss-found-in-children-taking-puberty-blockers.

15. Off-label prescriptions are legal and common. They involve doctors using drugs in ways the FDA did not determine to be safe and effective.

16. In the mid-twentieth century, Lupron was given to sex offenders and homosexual men and became known as "chemical castration." And, since the 1990s, doctors have prescribed Lupron to women with endometriosis.

17. Darcy Spears, "More Women Come Forward with Complaints about Lupron Side Effects," KNTV, February 12, 2019, https://www.ktnv.com/news/investigations/more-women-come

-forward-with-complaints-about-lupron-side-effects. Lupron is considered so "toxic" that it's not recommended for more than twelve months over the course of a lifetime.

18. Christina Jewett, "Drug Used to Halt Puberty in Children May Cause Lasting Health Problems," STAT, February 2, 2017, https://www.statnews.com/2017/02/02/lupron-puberty-children -health-problems/#:~:text=A%202003%20study%20in%20the,of %20growing%20a%20bit%20taller.

19. Simon Tegg, "Bone Health: Puberty Blockers Not 'Fully Reversible,'" October 20, 2021, https://genspect.org/bone-health -puberty-blockers-not-fully-reversible; https://segm.org/the_effect_of _puberty_blockers_on_the_accrual_of_bone_mass.

20. Jewett, "Drug Used to Halt Puberty in Children May Cause Lasting Health Problems."

21. Jane W. Robbins and Vernadette R. Broyles, "The Myth about Suicide and Gender Dysphoric Children," American College of Pediatricians study, https://acpeds.org/assets/for-GID-page-1-The -Myth-About-Suicide-and-Gender-Dysphoric-Children-handout .pdf.

22. Brandon Showalter, "UW Hid Concerns over Puberty Blockers in Trans Study amid Media Praise, Leaked Emails Show," *Christian Post,* August 26, 2022, https://www.christianpost.com /news/university-hid-concerns-about-transgender-study-emails-show .html?uid=*%7CUNIQID%7C*&utm_source= The+Christian +Post+List&utm_campaign=CP-Newsletter&utm_medium=email.

23. Thibault, *Transgender Ideology & Gender Dysphoria,* 490. Pediatric endocrinologist Norman Spack of Boston Children's Hospital said doctors aren't prescribing puberty blockers soon enough (478).

24. Anderson, *When Harry Became Sally,* 131.

25. Anderson, *When Harry Became Sally,* 122; Shrier, *Irreversible Damage,* 108.

26. Helen Joyce, *Trans: When Ideology Meets Reality* (London: Oneworld Publications, 2021), 83.

27. "Testosterone Hormones and Its Importance for Women," Hera Health Care, February 13, 2021, https://herahealthcare.com

/blog/testosterone-hormone-and-its-importance-for-women/#:~:text
=Studies%20have%20found%20that%20women,and%20more
%20fat%2Dfree%20mass.

28. Anderson, *When Harry Became Sally*, 130. Michael Monostra, "Erythrocytosis Present in 11% of Transgender Men Receiving Testosterone Therapy," Healio, February 19, 2021, https://www.healio.com/news/endocrinology/20210219/erythrocytosis -present-in-11-of-transgender-men-receiving-testosterone-therapy.

29. Joyce, *Trans*, 91.

30. Joyce, *Trans*, 90.

31. Shrier, *Irreversible Damage*, 155.

32. Shrier, *Irreversible Damage*, 155–56.

33. Anderson, *When Harry Became Sally*, 98. Eighty-seven percent of student health plans cover gender surgery.

34. Anderson, *When Harry Became Sally*, 99.

35. Abigail Shrier, "Top Trans Doctors Blow the Whistle on 'Sloppy' Care," Common Sense, October 4, 2021, https://www .commonsense.news/p/top-trans-doctors-blow-the-whistle.

36. Shrier, *Irreversible Damage*, 140.

37. Rikki Schlott, "'I Literally Lost Organs': Why Detransitioned Teens Regret Changing Genders," *New York Post*, June 18, 2022, https://nypost.com/2022/06/18/detransitioned-teens-explain-why -they-regret-changing-genders.

38. "What the Tavistock Clinic's Closure Means for the Trans Debate," *The Week*, August 2, 2022, https://www.theweek.co.uk /news/science-health/957525/tavistock-clinic-closure-trans-rights -debate; "World's Largest Pediatric Gender Clinic Shut Down Due to Poor Evidence, Risk of Harm and Operational Failures," Society for Evidence Based Gender Medicine, July 29, 2022, https://segm.org /UK_shuts-down-worlds-biggest-gender-clinic-for-kids.

39. Alia E. Dastagir, "Marsha Blackburn Asked Ketanji Brown Jackson to Define 'Woman.' Science Says There's No Simple Answer," *USA Today*, March 27, 2022, https://www.usatoday .com/story/life/health-wellness/2022/03/24/marsha-blackburn-asked -ketanji-jackson-define-woman-science/7152439001.

40. Dastagir, "Marsha Blackburn Asked Ketanji Brown Jackson to Define 'Woman.'"

41. Abigail Favale, *The Genesis of Gender* (Ignatius Press, July 11, 2022).

42. Abigail Favale, *The Genesis of Gender: A Christian Theory* (San Francisco: Ignatius Press, 2022), 106.

43. Favale, *The Genesis of Gender*, 103.

44. J. Budziszewski, *On the Meaning of Sex* (Wilmington, DE: ISI Books, 2012), 54. "Although bearing children is the most characteristic expression of motherhood, it is far from its only expression. . . . When I speak of failure [to nurture a child] . . . I am not speaking of giving up a child for adoption. My point is that potentiality for motherhood includes more than potentiality to give birth. That is why the woman who accepts the child is in that respect a true mother, too." Alice von Hildebrand remarked that, while not every woman is called to marry to have children, "every woman, whether married or unmarried, is called upon to be a biological, psychological or spiritual mother" (54).

45. Favale, *The Genesis of Gender*, 106.

46. Favale, *The Genesis of Gender*, 103.

47. Favale, *The Genesis of Gender*, 103.

48. Judith Butler, "Performative Acts and Gender Construction: An Essay in Phenomenology and Feminist Theory," *Theatre Journal*, 40, no. 4 (1998): 519–31.

49. Favale, *The Genesis of Gender*, 26.

50. Andrea Borghini, "Understand the Philosophical Theories of Nominalism and Realism," *ThoughtCo*, March 22, 2018, https://www.thoughtco.com/nominalism-vs-realism-2670598

51. Favale, *The Genesis of Gender*, 103.

52. Note the language of "gender confirmation surgeries" or achieving gender congruence.

53. Shrier, *Irreversible Damage*, 152.

54. *Teen Vogue*, Facebook, December 22, 2020, https://www.facebook.com/teenvogue/posts/your-no-nonsense-101-guide-to-masturbation-for-vagina-owners-/10158254546511312; Joyce, *Trans*, 144; Elizabeth T. H. Fontham, et al. "Cervical Cancer Screening

for Individuals at Average Risk: 2020 Guideline Update from the American Cancer Society," American Cancer Society, July 30, 2020, https://acsjournals.onlinelibrary.wiley.com/doi/full/10.3322/caac.21628.

55. Favale, *The Genesis of Gender*, 27, 131.

56. Shrier, *Irreversible Damage*.

57. "Am I Trans? Theory Testing. (What I've Learned over the Four Years I've Been Out and Scrolling through Trans Reddit," Reddit, accessed November 8, 2022, https://www.reddit.com/r/MtF/comments/re5k5u/am_i_trans_theory_testing_what_ive_learned_over.

58. Danielle Gray, "Tyra Skips Shaving Her Legs!" *Essence*, October 28, 2020, https://www.essence.com/articles/tyra-skips-shaving-her-legs.

59. Debra Soh, *The End of Gender: Debunking the Myths about Sex and Identity in Our Society* (New York: Threshold Editions, 2020), 43.

60. Soh, *The End of Gender*, 255.

61. Anderson, *When Harry Became Sally*, 104.

62. Favale, *The Genesis of Gender*, 138.

63. "Am I Trans Enough?," TransHub, accessed November 8, 2022, https://www.transhub.org.au/am-i-trans-enough.

64. Matt Walsh, "What Is a Woman?," *Daily Wire*, documentary, 2022.

65. Anderson, *When Harry Became Sally*, 101.

66. Anderson, *When Harry Became Sally*, 101.

67. Anderson, *When Harry Became Sally*, 100.

68. John D. Finley, "What Men and Women Mean to Us: A Philosophical Articulation," in *Sexual Identity: The Harmony of Philosophy, Science, and Revelation*, ed. John D. Finley (Steubenville, OH: Emmaus Road Publishing, 2022), 57.

69. John D. Finley, "What Men and Women Mean to Us," 64.

## Chapter 4: What: The Biological Differences Too Complex to Ignore

1. Quoted in Nancy R. Pearcey, *Love Thy Body* (Grand Rapids, MI: Baker Books, 2019), 196.

2. Debra Soh, *The End of Gender: Debunking the Myths about Sex and Identity in Our Society* (New York: Threshold Editions, 2020), 22.

3. See appendix A, "What about Intersex?"

4. Soh, *The End of Gender*, 29.

5. Colin Wright, "Sex Is Not a Spectrum," Reality's Last Stand, February 1, 2021, https://www.realityslaststand.com/p/sex-is-not-a -spectrum.

6. "Sex, Gender, and Transgender Experiences: Part 4— Brain Sex Theory," Center for Faith, Sexuality and Gender, August 6, 2019, https://www.centerforfaith.com/blog/sex-gender-and -transgender-experiences-part-4-brain-sex-theory.

7. Overall, for every brain region that showed even large sex differences, there was always overlap between males and females, confirming that **the human brain cannot**—at least for the measures observed here—be described as **"sexually dimorphic."** "Sex, Gender, and Transgender Experiences: Part 4–Brain Sex Theory," quoting Stuart Ritchie, et al. "Sex Differences in the Adult Human Brain: Evidence from 5216 UK Biobank Participants," *Cerebral Cortex* 28 (2018): 2959–75. Cf. Daphna Joel, et al. "Sex beyond the Genitalia: The Human Brain Mosaic," *PNAS* 112 (2015): 15468–73: "Human brains cannot be categorized into two distinct classes: male brain/female brain."

8. Larry Cahill, "Denying the Neuroscience of Sex Differences," *Quillette*, March 29, 2019, https://quillette.com/2019/03/29/denying -the-neuroscience-of-sex-differences. Cahill observes that when men and women really are different on average but we treat them like they are the same, it creates *inequality*, where men and women are not equally considered in light of their differences.

9. Google "male and female differences in the brain," and you'll find widespread disagreement between highly specialized professionals. It gets confusing fast—especially considering how many

studies have occurred since the cultural shift in views of gender. Even more confusing? Separating scientific research from social activism.

10. Stephanie Pappas, "Your Brain Is a Mosaic of Male and Female," *Live Science,* December 1, 2015, https://www.livescience.com/52941-brain-is-mix-male-and-female.html.

11. This differs from what's known as "brain sex" theory, which claims one's brain can have its own biological sex independent of one's anatomical sex [i.e., a female brain in a male body and *vice versa*].

12. Simon Baron-Cohen, *The Essential Difference: Men, Women and the Extreme Male Brain* (London: Penguin, 2012), 8.

13. "Intelligence in Men and Women Is a Gray and White Matter," Science Daily, January 22, 2005, sciencedaily.com/releases/2005/1/050121100142.htm.

14. Soh, *The End of Gender,* 17–18.

15. Louann Brizendine, *The Male Brain: A Breakthrough Understanding of How Men and Boys Think* (New York: Harmony Books, 2011), 13.

16. Louann Brizendine, *The Female Brain* (New York: Harmony Books, 2007), 36.

17. Soh, *The End of Gender,* 17. Portions of this chapter have been developed from an article I wrote for the Ethics and Religious Liberty Commission: Katie McCoy, "What Is a Woman?," ERLC, June 6, 2022, https://erlc.com/resource-library/articles/what-is-a-woman.

18. Brizendine, *The Female Brain,* 36.

19. Andrew J. Sodergren, "The Psychology of the Sexual Difference," in *Sexual Identity: The Harmony of Philosophy, Science, and Revelation,* ed. John Finley (Stuebenville, OH: Emmaus Road Publishing, 2022), 112.

20. Baron-Cohen, *The Essential Difference,* 5; Brizendine, *The Female Brain,* 36.

21. Baron-Cohen, *The Essential Difference,* 2, 23. It's important to note that Baron-Cohen doesn't claim that all men have "male brains" or that all women have "female brains" according to his

definitions. According to Baron-Cohen, men could have brains comparatively wired for empathy and women could have brains comparatively wired for systemizing. As with other researchers, he is noting averages and generalities. In Baron-Cohen's own words: "Just as empathizing is powerful enough to cope with the hundreds of emotions that exist, so systematizing is a process that can cope with an enormous number of systems. I will argue that, on average, males spontaneously systemize to a greater degree than do females again, note that I did not say 'all males' I am only talking about statistical averages, and we can learn from the exceptions to this rule, too" (3–4). "The central claim of this book is only that more males than females have a brain of type S [systemizer], and more females than males have a brain of type E [empathy]. . . . When I talk about sex differences in the mind, I am dealing only with statistical averages."

22. The male brain is hardwired for understanding and building systems. The parts of the brain related to mathematical abilities, spatial relationships, and perception of time and speed are significantly larger. Baron-Cohen defines *systemizing* as "the drive to analyze, explore, and construct a system. The systemizer intuitively figures out how things work, or extracts the underlying rules that govern the behavior of the system. This is done in order to understand and predict the system, or to invent a new one." Baron-Cohen, *The Essential Difference*, 3.

23. For the purpose of this work, I have focused my discussion on amplifying characteristics of the average female brain except where its contrast to the male brain is germane to the other topics addressed in this book. Systematizing is the drive to analyze, explore, and construct the system.

24. Soh, *The End of Gender*, 255; Sodergren, "The Psychology of the Sexual Difference," 114.

25. Brizendine, *The Female Brain*, 37–38.

26. Brizendine, *The Male Brain*, 12–13.

27. Brizendine, *The Female Brain*, 40.

28. Brizendine, *The Female Brain*, 41.

29. Bruce Goldman, "Two Minds: The Cognitive Differences between Men and Women," *Stanford Medicine: Sex, Gender, and Medicine* (Spring 2017): 16.

30. Brizendine, *The Female Brain*, 40. One study found three-year-old girls were able to read facial expressions as well as, or better than, five-year-old boys. Leonard Sax, *Why Gender Matters, 2nd ed.: What Parents and Teachers Need to Know about the Emerging Science of Sex Differences* (New York: Harmony Books, 2017), 87.

31. Brizendine, *The Female Brain*, 37–39, 44.

32. Brizendine, *The Female Brain*, 59.

33. Brizendine, *The Female Brain*, 42.

34. Anderson, *When Harry Became Sally*, 84; Soh, *The End of Gender*, 256; Goldman, "Two Minds," 14.

35. Baron-Cohen, *The Essential Difference*, 97; Sodergren, "The Psychology of the Sexual Difference," 114.

36. Sax, *Why Gender Matters*, 51.

37. Brizendine, *The Female Brain*, 44.

38. Brizendine, *The Female Brain*, 170.

39. Sahab Uddin, "Brain Chemistry and Sex Differences: Are Male and Female Brains Really Varied?," *Journal of Neuroscience and Neuropharmacology* 4, no. 1 (1998): 1. "7 Differences between Male and Female Brains," Amen Clinic, September 22, 2021, https://www.amenclinics.com/blog/7-differences-between-male-and -female-brains.

40. Richard Lippa, *Gender, Nature, and Nurture*, 2nd ed. (Mahwah, NJ: Lawrence Erlbaum, 2005), 33, 101; Brizendine, *The Female Brain*, 62; Soh, *The End of Gender*, 45. Females are also typically stronger at language performance. Stephen Furlich, *Sex Talk: How Biological Sex Influences Gender Communication Differences throughout Life's Stages* (New Providence, NJ: Bowker, 2021), Kindle Loc. 1034.

41. Baron-Cohen, *The Essential Difference*, 102.

42. Furlich, *Sex Talk*, Kindle Loc. 964.

43. Brizendine, *The Female Brain*, 60.

44. Cahill, "Denying the Neuroscience of Sex Differences." "The enormous power of animal research, of course, is that it can

establish sex influences in particular on mammalian brain function (such as sex differences in risk-taking, play behavior, and responses to social defeat as just three examples) that cannot be explained by human culture, (although they may well be influenced in humans by culture)."

45. Sodergren, "The Psychology of the Sexual Difference," 116–17.

46. Goldman, "Two Minds."

47. University of California, Irvine, "Intelligence in Men and Women Is a Gray and White Matter," *ScienceDaily*, January 22, 2005, www.sciencedaily.com/releases/2005/01/050121100142.htm; Furlich, *Sex Talk*, Kindle Loc. 982.

48. Furlich, *Sex Talk*, Kindle Loc. 982.

49. University of California, Irvine, "Intelligence in Men and Women Is a Gray and White Matter."

50. Furlich, *Sex Talk*, Kindle Loc. 982.

51. University of California, Irvine, "Intelligence in Men and Women Is a Gray and White Matter."

52. Alexei Oreskovic, "A Senior Engineer at Google Wrote a Controversial Diversity Manifesto and Employees Are Furious," *Business Insider*, August 5, 2017, https://www.businessinsider.com /google-engineer-anti-diversity-manifesto-causes-uproar-2017-8.

53. "Who Was Katherine Johnson?," NASA, February 24, 2020, https://www.nasa.gov/audience/forstudents/k-4/stories/nasa-knows/ who-was-katherine-johnson-k4.

54. Larry Cahill, "His Brain, Her Brain," *Scientific American* (May 2005): 43. Larry Cahill, "Equal ≠ The Same: Sex Differences in the Human Brain," National Library of Medicine, April 1, 2014, https://www.ncbi.nlm.nih.gov/pmc/articles/PMC4087190.

55. Goldman, "Two Minds," 14.

56. Furlich, *Sex Talk*, Kindle Loc. 1005.

57. Furlich, *Sex Talk*, Kindle Loc. 1005.

58. Jake Thibault, *Transgender Ideology & Gender Dysphoria: A Catholic Response* (Providence, RI: Maryvale Catholic Press, 2021), 394.

59. Brizendine, *The Female Brain*, 60, 96.

60. Baron-Cohen, *The Essential Difference*, 26.

61. Brizendine, *The Female Brain*, 61.

62. Brizendine, *The Female Brain*, 45.

63. Brizendine, *The Female Brain*, 67.

64. Brizendine, *The Female Brain*, 45.

65. Brizendine, *The Female Brain*, 61.

66. Brizendine, *The Female Brain*, 68.

67. Brizendine, *The Female Brain*, 44.

68. Sax, *Why Gender Matters*, 75.

69. Sax, *Why Gender Matters*, 76.

70. Baron-Cohen, *The Essential Difference*, 26.

71. Brizendine, *The Female Brain*, 62.

72. Baron-Cohen, *The Essential Difference*, 52.

73. Sax, *Why Gender Matters*, 74–75.

74. Brizendine, *The Female Brain*, 64–65.

75. Sax, *Why Gender Matters*, 75.

76. Goldman, "Two Minds."

77. Goldman, "Two Minds," 14.

78. Mayo Clinic Staff, "Depression in Women: Understanding the Gender Gap," Mayo Clinic, accessed November 8, 2022, https://www.mayoclinic.org/diseases-conditions/depression/in-depth/depression/art-20047725; Dale Vernor, "PTSD Is More Likely in Women than Men," *NAMI*, October 8, 2019; https://www.nami.org/Blogs/NAMI-Blog/October-2019/PTSD-is-More-Likely-in-Women-Than-Men.

79. Paul Albert, "Why Is Depression More Prevalent in Women?," *Journal of Psychiatry and Neuroscience* 40, no. 4 (2015): 218–21, https://www.ncbi.nlm.nih.gov/pmc/articles/PMC4478054. Women are also more prone than men to all anxiety-related disorders. Goldman, "Two Minds."

80. Mary V. Seeman, "Psychopathology in Women and Men: Focus on Female Hormones," *American Journal of Psychiatry*, vol. 154, no. 12 (1997): 1641–47, https://ajp.psychiatryonline.org/doi/full/10.1176/ajp.154.12.1641?mobileUi=0; Budziszewski, *On the Meaning of Sex*, 47.

81. "Study Finds Sex Differences in Mental Illness," *American Journal of Psychiatry*, 2011, https://www.apa.org/news/press/releases/2011/08/mental-illness.

82. "Estrogen and Neuroprotection: From Clinical Observation to Molecular Mechanism," *Dialogues in Clinical Neuroscience* 4, no. 2 (2002), https://www.tandfonline.com/doi/full/10.31887/DCNS.2002.4.2/ddubal#:~:text=Studies%20demonstrate%20that%20estrogen%20acts,the%20onset%20of%20neurodegenerative%20conditions.

83. Siri Carpenter, "Does Estrogen Protect Memory?," *American Psychological Association* 32, no. 1 (2001), https://www.apa.org/monitor/jan01/estrogen; Seeman, "Psychopathology in Women and Men."

84. Carol Vlassoff, "Gender Differences in Determinants and Consequences of Health and Illness," *Journal of Health, Population and Nutrition* 25, no. 1 (2007): 47–61, https://www.ncbi.nlm.nih.gov/pmc/articles/PMC3013263.

85. Gail D. Anderson, "Gender Differences in Pharmalogical Response," *National Library of Medicine*, 83 (2008): 1–10, https://pubmed.ncbi.nlm.nih.gov/18929073.

86. Catherine Erlinger, "Heart Attack: Men vs. Women," The Heart Foundation, March 29, 2017, https://theheartfoundation.org/2017/03/29/heart-attack-men-vs-women.

87. Katherine Rosman, "Read It and Weep, Crybabies," *Wall Street Journal*, May 4, 2011, https://www.wsj.com/articles/SB10001424052748703922804576300903183512350.

88. Sax, *Why Gender Matters*, 18.

89. "Biological Sex Differences: Bones & Muscles," Fair Play for Women, July 7, 2017, https://fairplayforwomen.com/biological-sex-differences/#:~:text=Is%20There%20A%20Difference%20Between,the%20composition%20of%20their%20muscles.

90. Melanie Schoor, et al., "Sex Differences in Body Composition and Association with Cardiometabolic Risk," *Biology of Sex Differences* 9, no. 28 (2018). Body composition differs between men and women, with women having proportionally more fat mass and men more muscle mass.

91. "Biological Sex Differences: Bones & Muscles."

92. Tia Ghose, "Women in Combat: Physical Differences May Mean Uphill Battle," *Live Science,* December 7, 2015, https://www .livescience.com/52998-women-combat-gender-differences.html.

93. Frederic Delavier, "Learn Why Women Carry More Fat Than Men," Human Kinetics, accessed November 8, 2022, https:// us.humankinetics.com/blogs/excerpt/learn-why-women-carry-more -fat-than-men.

94. K. M. Haizlip et al., "Sex-Based Differences in Skeletal Muscle Kinetics and Fiber-Type Composition," *Physiology* 30, no. 1 (2015): 30–39. In January 2015, *Physiology,* the official journal of the American Physiological Society, published a study on the differences in skeletal muscle kinetics between the sexes. It identified more than three thousand genes expressed differently in male and female skeletal muscles, those movement-propelling muscles connected to the skeleton.

95. Dan Ketchum, "Is There a Difference between Male and Female Muscles," Livestrong, June 17, 2019, https://www.livestrong .com/article/355987-female-male-muscles.

96. Sodergren, "The Psychology of the Sexual Difference," 107–8.

97. Budziszewski, *On the Meaning of Sex,* 42.

98. Nancy Pearcey, *Love Thy Body,* 205.

## Chapter 5: Who: The Theological Meaning of Female Identity

1. John D. Finley, "What Men and Women Mean to Us: A Philosophical Articulation," in *Sexual Identity: The Harmony of Philosophy, Science, and Revelation,* ed. John DeSilva Finley (Steubenville, OH: Emmaus Road Publishing, 2022), 62.

2. Finley, "What Men and Women Mean to Us," 59.

3. John Paul II, *Theology of the Body in Simple Language* (Philokalia Books, 2008), 29.

4. John Paul II, *Theology of the Body in Simple Language,* 17.

5. Karl Barth, *Church Dogmatics: The Doctrine of Creation,* vol. 3, part 4 (New York: T&T Clark, 1961), 163.

6. Dietrich Bonhoffer, *Creation and Fall: A Theological Exposition of Genesis 1–3*, ed. John W. deGruchy, trans. Douglas Stephen Bax (Minneapolis: Fortress Press, 1997), 64–65.

7. Timothy C. Tennent, *For the Body* (Grand Rapids, MI: Zondervan Reflective, 2020), 19.

8. Tennent, *For the Body*, 19.

9. John F. Kilner, *Dignity and Destiny* (Grand Rapids, MI: Eerdmans, 2015), 132.

10. Matthew Schmitz, "N.T. Wright on Gay Marriage," *First Things,* June 11, 2014, https://www.firstthings.com/blogs/firstthoughts/2014/06/n-t-wrights-argument-against-same-sex-marriage.

11. Andrew J. Sodergren, "The Psychology of the Sexual Difference," in *Sexual Identity: The Harmony of Philosophy, Science, and Revelation*, ed. John DeSilva Finley (Steubenville, OH: Emmaus Road Publishing, 2022), 106.

12. Brett McCracken, "The Beauty of Complementarity Goes beyond Gender," The Gospel Coalition, July 28, 2018, https://www.thegospelcoalition.org/article/beauty-complementarity-goes-beyond-gender.

13. Nancy Pearcey, *Love Thy Body* (Grand Rapids, MI: Baker Books, 2018), 74.

14. Abigail Favale, *The Genesis of Gender: A Christian Theory* (San Francisco: Ignatius Press, 2022), 34–35.

15. Ryan T. Anderson, *When Harry Became Sally: Responding to the Transgender Movement* (New York: Encounter Books, 2018), 79, 81.

16. Anderson, *When Harry Became Sally*, 80.

17. Tennent, *For the Body*, 14.

18. Favale, *The Genesis of Gender*, 32–33, 35.

19. Tennent, *For the Body*, 15.

20. Andrew T. Walker, *God and the Transgender Debate: What Does the Bible Actually Say about Gender Identity?*, expanded and updated (Epsom, Surrey, UK: Good Book Company, 2022), 50, cf. 50–54.

21. Tennent, *For the Body*, 17.

22. Pearcey, *Love Thy Body*, 40.

23. Pearcey, *Love Thy Body*, 35.

24. John Paul II, *Theology of the Body*, 140.

25. Pearcey, *Love Thy Body*, 35–36.

26. "If our bodies are untrustworthy and only serve to mask the true self that is within, then the incarnation of the second person of the trinity as Jesus of Nazareth cannot be trusted as a reliable means for God's most profound self-disclosure in history." Tennent, *For the Body*, 25.

27. Pearcey, *Love Thy Body*, 34.

28. Pearcey, *Love Thy Body*, 34.

29. John Paul II, *Theology of the Body*, 141.

30. Pearcey, *Love Thy Body*, 38.

31. Pearcey, *Love Thy Body*, 31, 33–34.

32. Quoted in Tennent, *For the Body*, 20.

33. Tennent, *For the Body*, 14–15.

34. Favale, *The Genesis of Gender*, 131.

35. Jonathan Merritt, "Nancy Pearcey and Jonathan Merritt Spar on the Hottest of Hot Topics," Religion News Service, January 26, 2018, https://religionnews.com/2018/01/26/from-secularism-to-sexuality-nancy-pearcey-and-i-spar-on-the-hottest-of-hot-topics.

36. Preston Sprinkle, *Embodied: Transgender Identities, the Church, and What the Bible Has to Say* (Colorado Springs: David C. Cook, 2021), 24.

37. Sprinkle, *Embodied*, 23.

38. John Mark Comer, *Live No Lies: Recognize and Resist the Three Enemies That Sabotage Your Peace* (Colorado Springs: Waterbrook, 2021), 61.

39. Comer, *Live No Lies*, 64.

40. Comer, *Live No Lies*, 57.

41. Comer, *Live No Lies*, 65.

42. Comer, *Live No Lies*, 233.

43. Walker, *God and the Transgender Debate*, 80.

44. Walker, *God and the Transgender Debate*, 70.

45. The symptoms of gender dysphoria may be occasioned by or the result of sin from which we can turn away and find forgiveness.

And it can be a coping mechanism to redirect suffering from someone else's sin. Even so, the psychological distress of gender dysphoria is not sin in itself.

46. Tim Keller, *Walking with God through Pain and Suffering*
(New York: Penguin Books, 2013), 47.

47. Walker, *God and the Transgender Debate*, 112.

48. Pearcey, *Love Thy Body*, 197.

## Chapter 6: Around the Corner: What You Can't Afford Not to Know

1. Sarah Eekhoff Zylstra, "Transformation of a Transgender
Teen," The Gospel Coalition, July 6, 2022, https://www.thegospel
coalition.org/article/transformation-transgender-teen.

2. Simon Baron-Cohen, *The Essential Difference: Men, Women
and the Extreme Male Brain* (London: Penguin, 2012).

3. Nancy R. Pearcey, *Love Thy Body* (Grand Rapids, MI: Baker
Books, 2019), 218.

4. Preston Sprinkle, *Embodied: Transgender Identities, the
Church, and What the Bible Has to Say* (Colorado Springs, CO:
David C. Cook, 2021), 152.

5. Katie McCoy, "An Executive Order Marginalizing Women
and Girls," *World Magazine*, January 29, 2021, https://wng.org/articles
/an-executive-order-marginalizing-women-and-girls-1617296647.

6. Bethany Mandel, "Wi Spa Indecency Case Exposes the Anti-
Woman Thrust of Trans Ideology," *New York Post*, September 2,
2021, https://nypost.com/2021/09/02/wi-spa-indecency-case-exposes
-the-anti-woman-thrust-of-trans-ideology.

7. Transgender persons have also been horrifically assaulted in
prisons as well. The focus of my research is on how trans ideologies
are affecting females. Zachary Rogers, "Trans Prisoner Moved from
Women's Prison after Impregnating Other Inmates, Report Says,"
KATV, July 18, 2022, https://katv.com/news/nation-world/trans
-inmate-transferred-moved-from-womens-prison-after-impregnating
-2-report-says-transgender-prison-new-jersey-edna-mahan-demi
-minor; Caroline Downey, "Male Inmate Convicted of Raping
Female at Rikers Island's Women's Facility," *National Review*,

April 26, 2022, https://www.yahoo.com/entertainment/transgender
-inmate-convicted-raping-female-225931569.html?guccounter
=1&guce_referrer=aHR0cHM6Ly93d3cuZ29vZ2xlLmNvbS88
&guce_referrer_sig=AQAAAMq0msTB0ZViYAweUNt0fZMs2L
s8Zaqn4RIGyjjUNB0gGQB1VitC99r1Btda_6IDPJMhMmYLiHp
YkvKvVoQzBOQeNWHx5jJX2Qtn8YqEy-S2uK1Q83C9q1jtC_
Ana4Jxp1d6haZBeXwYFGOeJzTjLy_nRwSkaZRDy5Cb-6QqiCup;
Matt Masterson, "Lawsuit: Female Prisoner Says She Was Raped
by Transgender Inmate," WTTW, February 19, 2020, https://news
.wttw.com/2020/02/19/lawsuit-female-prisoner-says-she-was-raped
-transgender-inmate.

8. Madeleine Kerns, "Women-Only Rape-Relief Shelter
Defunded, Then Vandalized," *National Review*, August 28, 2019,
https://www.nationalreview.com/2019/08/women-only-rape-relief
-shelter-defunded-then-vandalized.

9. Jean C. Lloyd, "Why a Generation of Girls Is Fleeing
Womanhood," *Public Discourse*, August 10, 2020, https://www
.thepublicdiscourse.com/2020/08/69452.

10. Abigail Shrier, "The Book Silicon Valley Tried to Kill:
Abigail Shrier's Investigation into the Exploding Numbers of Girls
Wanting to Change Sex Has Caused an Outcry in America—but
Her Story Must Be Heard," *Daily Mail*, January 2, 2021, https://
www.dailymail.co.uk/news/article-9106895/ABIGAIL-SHRIERS
-investigation-exploding-numbers-girls-wanting-change-sex.html.
Lloyd, "Why a Generation of Girls Is Fleeing Womanhood."

11. Content warning: Genevieve Gluck, "Sissy Porn, The
Gender Movement's Dirty Secret," The Glinner Update, November
29, 2020, https://grahamlinehan.substack.com/p/sissy-porn-the
-gender-movements-dirty.

12. Jake Thibault, *Transgender Ideology & Gender Dysphoria: A
Catholic Response* (Providence, RI: Maryvale Catholic Press, 2021),
469.

13. Gluck, "Sissy Porn."

14. Thibault, *Transgender Ideology & Gender Dysphoria*, 465–49.

15. Ashley Sadler, "'Queer Neurodivergent' Teacher Brags
about Indoctrinating Small Children into Gender Ideology,"

*LifeSite*, August 19, 2021, https://www.lifesitenews.com/news/queer
-neurodivergent-teacher-brags-about-indoctrinating-small-children
-into-gender-ideology.

16. Libs of TikTok, Twitter, April 10, 2022, https://twitter.com/
libsoftiktok/status/1513046467333689344.

17. "Genderbread Person v2.1," The Genderbread Person,
accessed November 9, 2022, https://www.genderbread.org/resource
/genderbread-person-v2-1; Staff, "Parent References 'GenderBread
Person' in Public Testimony on Parental Rights in Education Bill,"
March 3, 2022, Tallahassee Reports, https://tallahasseereports
.com/2022/03/03/parent-references-genderbread-person-in-public
-testimony-on-parental-rights-in-education-bill; Rick Gonzales,
"What Is The Genderbread Person and How Is It Being Used
in Schools?," Go2Tutors, https://go2tutors.com/what-is-the
-genderbread-person-and-how-is-it-being-used-in-schools.

18. Henry Olsen, "California Wants to Teach Kindergartners
about Gender Identity. Seriously," *Washington Post*, May 13, 2019,
https://www.washingtonpost.com/opinions/2019/05/13/california
-wants-teach-kindergartners-about-gender-identity-seriously.

19. Joy Pullman, "How Illinois Schools Teach Preschoolers
to Celebrate Transgenderism," *The Federalist*, October 9, 2019,
https://thefederalist.com/2019/10/09/how-illinois-schools-teach
-preschoolers-to-celebrate-transgenderism.

20. "Fostering Inclusive Classrooms," Pride and Less Prejudice,
accessed November 9, 2022, https://www.prideandlessprejudice.org;
Libs of TikTok, July 16, 2022, https://twitter.com/libsoftiktok/status
/1537511540969984002?s=20&t=G_t7PZRuzhHPTumDW_RDug;
Libs of TikTok; June 23, 2022, https://twitter.com/libsoftiktok/status
/1540076065879621636?s=20&t=G_t7PZRuzhHPTumDW_RDug;
Libs of TikTok; August 8, 2022, https://twitter.com/libsoftiktok
/status/1556729089364566016?s=20&t=G_t7PZRuzhHPTumDW
_RDug.

21. Betsy McCaughey, "How Public Schools Brainwash
Young Kids with Harmful Transgender Ideology," *New York
Post*, December 22, 2021, https://nypost.com/2021/12/22/how-public
-schools-brainwash-young-kids-with-harmful-transgender-ideology;

Brian Melley, "Mother: Teachers Manipulated Child to Change Gender Identity," ABC News, January 21, 2022, https://abcnews .go.com/US/wireStory/mother-teachers-manipulated-child-change -gender-identity-82405978.

22. Aila Slisco, "Outraged Parents' Lawsuit Alleges Gender Dysphoria Lessons Given to Kids," *Newsweek*, June 6, 2022, https://www.newsweek.com/outraged-parents-lawsuit-alleges-gender -dysphoria-lesson-given-kids-1714899.

23. Alastair Talbot, "North Carolina Preschool Teacher Resigns after She Was Caught Using Unauthorized LGBTQ-Themed Flashcards Showing a Pregnant Man to Teach Three- and Four-year-old Children about Colors," *DailyMail*, May 31, 2022, https://www.dailymail.co.uk/news/article-10872475/North -Carolina-preschool-teacher-RESIGNS-condemned-using-LGBTQ -flashcards-class.html.

24. "Pink, Blue, and Purple" *Advocates for Youth*, https://www .advocatesforyouth.org/wp-content/uploads/2021/08/3Rs_Grade1 _PinkBluePurple_2021.pdf.

25. "Pink, Blue, and Purple"; Laura Meckler, "Gender Identity Lessons, Banned in Some Schools, Are Rising in Others," *Washington Post*, June 3, 2022, https://www.washingtonpost.com /education/2022/06/03/schools-gender-identity-transgender-lessons.

26. Katie Forster, "Secret of the Teenage Brain," *The Guardian*, January 15, 2015, https://www.theguardian.com/lifeandstyle/2015 /jan/25/secrets-of-the-teenage-brain.

27. Fresh Air, "Why Teens Are Impulsive, Addiction-Prone and Should Protect Their Brains," NPR, January 28, 2015, https://www .npr.org/sections/health-shots/2015/01/28/381622350/why-teens-are -impulsive-addiction-prone-and-should-protect-their-brains.

28. Dr. Francis E. Jensen and Amy Ellis Nutt, "Teen Girls Have Different Brains: Gender, Neuroscience and the Truth about Adolescence," *Salon*, January 3, 2015, https://www.salon.com/2015 /01/03/teen_girls_have_different_brains_gender_neuroscience_and _the_truth_about_adolescence.

29. Jared Eckert, "Tech and Trans Confusion," The Heritage Foundation, June 21, 2022, https://www.heritage.org/gender/commentary/tech-and-trans-confusion.

30. Eckert, "Tech and Trans Confusion."

31. Canela Lopez, "6 Tech Executives Who Raise Their Kids Tech-Free or Seriously Limit Their Screen Time," Insider, March 5, 2020, https://www.businessinsider.com/tech-execs-screen-time-children-bill-gates-steve-jobs-2019-9; Olivia Rudgard, "The Tech Moguls Who Invented Social Media Have Banned Their Children from It," Independent.ie, November 6, 2018, https://www.independent.ie/life/family/parenting/the-tech-moguls-who-invented-social-media-have-banned-their-children-from-it-37494367.html.

32. David French, "Chelsea Manning and the Problem with Pronouns," National Review, May 19, 2017, https://www.nationalreview.com/2017/05/chelsea-manning-man-masculine-pronouns-transgender-law-title-ix.

33. "Should I Call Someone by their Preferred Pronouns?," RZIM HQ, YouTube, April 9, 2019, https://www.youtube.com/watch?v=4ur-lfYF4dc.

34. Abigail Favale, The Genesis of Gender: A Christian Theory (San Francisco: Ignatius Press, 2022), 26.

35. Andrew Walker, "Capitulation to Falsehood Is Not Christian Kindness," American Reformer, August 19, 2022, https://americanreformer.org/2022/08/christians-volunteering-pronouns.

36. Stella Morbito, "A De-Sexed Society Is a De-Humanized Society," Public Discourse, May 25, 2016, https://thepublicdiscourse.com/2016/05/17041.

37. Jonathan Merritt, "Nancy Pearcey and Jonathan Merritt Spar on the Hottest of Hot Topics," Religion News Service, January 26, 2018, https://religionnews.com/2018/01/26/from-secularism-to-sexuality-nancy-pearcey-and-i-spar-on-the-hottest-of-hot-topics.

38. Jeff Johnston, "Canadian Dad Sentenced for Trying to Protect Daughter from Transgender Medical Procedures," Daily Citizen, April 20, 2021, https://dailycitizen.focusonthefamily.com/canadian-dad-sentenced-for-trying-to-protect-daughter-from-transgender-medical-procedures.

## Chapter 7: Looking Back and Moving Forward

1. Jon Tyson, *Beautiful Resistance: The Joy of Conviction in a Culture of Compromise* (Colorado Springs: Multnomah, 2020), 9.

2. "These ideas *became* traditional because so many people realized they led to human flourishing. But in our post-Christian, deconstructionist zeitgeist, they've become radical yet again." John Mark Comer, *Live No Lies: Recognize and Resist the Three Enemies That Sabotage Your Peace* (Colorado Springs: WaterBrook, 2021), 234.

3. Domitilla Campanile, Filippo Carlà-Uhink, and Margherita Facella, eds., *TransAntiquity: Cross-Dressing and Transgender Dynamics in the Ancient World* (London: Routledge, 2019).

4. David Watson, "Elagabalus," *World History Encyclopedia*, October 21, 2013, https://www.worldhistory.org/Elagabalus; Abigail Hudson, "LGBTQIA+ History Month—Elagabalus, the Trans Emperor of Rome?—Ollie Burns," University of Birmingham, February 18, 2021, https://blog.bham.ac.uk/historybham/lgbtqia-history-month-elagabalus-the-trans-emperor-of-rome-ollie-burns; "Was Elagabalus Rome's First Transgender Emperor?," History, https://www.history.co.uk/articles/was-elagabalus-rome-s-first-transgender-emperor.

5. "The Galli: Breaking Roman Gender Norms," English Heritage, accessed November 23, 2022, https://www.english-heritage.org.uk/learn/histories/lgbtq-history/the-galli/#:~:text=The%20Galli%20were%20priests%20in,dressed%20exclusively%20in%20women's%20clothing.

6. Kyle Harper, *From Sin to Shame* (Cambridge, MA: Harvard University Press, 2013), 15–16. "The progressive realization of its injustice is a privileged index of Christianization."

7. Chris Hayden, "Untrue to State That St Patrick Brought Misery to Ireland," *The Irish Times*, March 17, 2015, https://www.irishtimes.com/opinion/untrue-to-state-that-st-patrick-brought-misery-to-ireland-1.2141959; "St. Patrick Ended Child Sacrifice in Ireland. Will Fine Gael Bring It Back?," Josh Craddock, The Stream, March 17, 2018, https://stream.org/st-patrick-ended-child-sacrifice.

8. Preston Sprinkle, *Embodied: Transgender Identities, the Church, and What the Bible Has to Say* (Colorado Springs: David C. Cook, 2021), 20.

9. Comer, *Live No Lies,* 57.

10. 1 Corinthians 13; John 8:32.

11. "Why Is Art Important?," Eden Gallery, March 1, 2022, https://www.eden-gallery.com/news/why-is-art-important.

## Appendix A: What about Intersex?

1. Intersex is usually the "I" in the gender acronym LGBTQIA.

2. Debra Soh, *The End of Gender: Debunking the Myths about Sex and Identity in Our Society* (New York: Threshold Editions, 2020), 23.

3. Jake Thibault, *Transgender Ideology & Gender Dysphoria: A Catholic Response* (Providence, RI: Maryvale Catholic Press, 2021), 284.

4. Nancy Pearcey, *Love Thy Body* (Grand Rapids, MI: Baker Books, 2018), 219.

5. Preston Sprinkle, *Embodied: Transgender Identities, the Church, and What the Bible Has to Say* (Colorado Springs: David C. Cook, 2021), 118.

6. Sprinkle, *Embodied,* 118.

7. Soh, *The End of Gender,* 22.

8. Sprinkle, *Embodied,* 114.

9. Jennifer Anne Cox, *Intersex in Christ: Ambiguous Biology and the Gospel* (Eugene, OR: Cascade Books, 2018), Kindle Loc. 546.

10. Fima Lifshitz, ed., *Pediatric Endocrinology,* 5th ed., vol. 1 (New York: Informa Healthcare, 2007), 382. When an intersex child is born, doctors will assess the anatomy of the sex organs then recommend treatments and measures according to "the likely cosmetic appearance of the reconstructed genitalia, on the potential for normal sex steroid secretion at puberty, on the potential for normal sexual intercourse, and on the potential for fertility."

11. Lifshitz, *Pediatric Endocrinology.*

12. Cox, *Intersex in Christ,* 637–38.

13. "Male and Female He Created Them": *Towards a Path of Dialogue on the Question of Gender Theory in Education* (Vatican City, 2019), sec. 26.

14. Thibault, *Transgender Ideology & Gender Dysphoria*, 293.

15. Cox, *Intersex in Christ*, 472; Pearcey, *Love Thy Body*, 222.

16. Cox, *Intersex in Christ*, 1089.

17. Cox, *Intersex in Christ*, 969.

18. Pearcey, *Love Thy Body*, 220.

19. Megan K. DeFranza, *Sex Difference in Christian Theology: Male, Female and Intersex in the Image of God* (Grand Rapids, MI: Eerdmans, 2015), 66.

20. DeFranza, *Sex Difference in Christian Theology*, 65.

21. DeFranza, *Sex Difference in Christian Theology*, 287.

22. DeFranza, *Sex Difference in Christian Theology*, 286.

23. DeFranza, *Sex Difference in Christian Theology*, 287.

24. Megan DeFranza, "Good News for Gender Minorities," in *Understanding Transgender Identities* (Grand Rapids, MI: Baker Academic, 2019).

25. "Megan DeFranza | Eerdmans Author Interview Series," Eerdmans, March 16, 2015, YouTube video, https://www.youtube.com/watch?v=2qka0U7_ZO0&fbclid=IwAR3lfZemWrx28rOpmo3XQ1az53cxPv3gBUWDofD_H8LAEOGBuHQNSznL1boIt.

26. "Megan DeFranza | Eerdmans Author Interview Series."

27. Preston Sprinkle, "What Is Intersex? Julie Zaagman and Dr. Sam Ashton," *Theology in the Raw*, June 16, 2022.

28. Sprinkle, "What Is Intersex?" In the words of a Christian intersex woman interviewed: "My function within creation is different. I'm not a swamp or a marsh. I have a soul." Moreover, as Nancy Pearcey observes, creation does indeed include great variety, but there are also mutations that disrupt how creation was intended to function. We can acknowledge when something is not typical, healthy, or able to function as designed without being unloving or dismissive of intersex people's pain. Pearcey, *Love Thy Body*, 220.

29. Alesdair H. Ittleson, "Attacks on Trans Athletes Are Also Attacks on Intersex People," American Civil Liberties Union, October 23, 2020, https://www.aclu.org/news/lgbtq-rights

/attacks-on-trans-athletes-are-also-an-attack-on-intersex-people. The American Civil Liberties Union conflates the two outright, claiming an "attack" on transgender athletes is an attack against the intersex community.

30. "Understanding Intersex and Transgender Communities," InterAct: Advocates for Intersex Youth, accessed November 23, 2022, https://interactadvocates.org/wp-content/uploads/2016/05/LavLaw-Trans-and-Intersex-Fact-Sheet.pdf. "While intersex individuals are forced to undergo medically unnecessary surgeries in infancy, transgender individuals are often denied desired medical treatment in adolescence and beyond. Both communities grapple with a loss of decision-making authority over their own bodies."

31. Pearcey, *Love Thy Body*, 219.

32. Ryan T. Anderson, *When Harry Became Sally: Responding to the Transgender Movement* (New York: Encounter Books, 2018), 92. "Not all intersex people are trans and not all trans people are intersex." Soh, *The End of Gender*, 22.

33. Anderson, *When Harry Became Sally*, 88. See also Sprinkle, *Embodied*, 122.

34. Sprinkle, *Embodied*, 114.

## Appendix B: Is Gender Dysphoria Brain Based?

1. J. Alan Branch, *Affirming God's Image: Addressing the Transgender Question with Science and Scripture* (Bellingham, WA: Lexham Press, 2019), 57. Your height and skin color, for instance, are determined by more than one gene, whereas eye color and freckles are determined by a single gene.

2. Branch, *Affirming God's Image*, 58.

3. Branch, *Affirming God's Image*, 58.

4. The cluster is called the third interstitial nuclei of the anterior hypothalamus (INAH 3).

5. John S. Feinberg and Paul D. Feinberg, *Ethics for a Brave New World* (Wheaton, IL: Crossway, 2010), 369.

6. Feinberg and Feinberg, *Ethics for a Brave New World*, 370.

7. Branch, *Affirming God's Image*, 80.

8. Julie Bakker, "Brain Structure and Function in Gender Dysphoria," Endocrine Abstracts 56 (2018): S30.3, https://doi.org/10.1530/endoabs.56.S30.3.

9. European Society of Endocrinology, "Transgender Brains Are More Like Their Desired Gender from an Early Age," ScienceDaily, May 24, 2018, www.sciencedaily.com/releases/2018/05/180524112351.htm; Mike Colagrossi, "Transgender Brains More Closely Resemble Brains of the Sex They Align With, Rather Than What They're Born With," BigThink, June 3, 2018, https://bigthink.com/mind-brain/transgender-brains-more-closely-resemble-brains-of-the-sex-they-align-with-rather-than-what-they-were-born-with.

10. Brandon Showalter, "Study Showing Brains Differ for Gender Dysphoria Doesn't Prove Transgenderism Innate, Experts Say," *Christian Post,* June 4, 2018, https://www.christianpost.com/news/study-showing-brains-differ-gender-dysphoria-doesnt-prove-transgenderism-innate-experts.html.

11. Branch, *Affirming God's Image,* 58–60. A 2009 Australian study of 112 male-to-female (MtF) transsexuals claimed to find a connection, but they couldn't replicate the findings of the 2005 Swedish study. A 2009 Japanese study examined 74 MtF and 168 female-to-male (FtM) transsexuals attempting to establish a link between receptors in transsexuals. Its authors reported their findings did not yield "any evidence that genetic variants of sex hormone-related genes confer individual susceptibility to MtF or FtM transsexualism." The same can be said for studies analyzing the CYP17 gene, an enzyme that contributes to forming sex hormones and the SRD5A2 gene, which gives cellular information to produce hormone receptors.

12. Jiska Ristori, Carlotta Cocchetti, Alessia Romani, Francesca Mazzoli, Linda Vignozzi, Mario Maggi, and Alessandra Daphne Fisher, "Brain Sex Differences Related to Gender Identity Development: Genes or Hormones?," *International Journal of Molecular Sciences* 21, no. 6 (2020): 2123, https://doi.org/10.3390/ijms21062123.

13. Branch, *Affirming God's Image,* 67.

14. Branch, *Affirming God's Image,* 79.

15. Kendra Cherry, "What Is Neuroplasticity?," VeryWellMind, February 18, 2022, https://www.verywellmind.com/what-is-brain -plasticity-2794886#:~:text=Neuroplasticity%20is%20the%20 brain's%20ability,brain%20is%20similar%20to%20plastic.

16. Lara Boyd, "After Watching This, Your Brain Will Not Be the Same," TEDx Talks, December 15, 2015, https://www.youtube .com/watch?time_continue=39&v=LNHBMFCzznE&feature =emb_title.

17. Showalter, "Study Showing Brains Differ for Gender Dysphoria Doesn't Prove Transgenderism Innate, Experts Say."

18. "Inside NFT, a Rehab Helping Paralyzed People Move Again," *Today*, December 21, 2018, https://www.today.com /video/inside-nft-a-rehab-helping-paralyzed-people-move-again -1404114499556.

19. Showalter, "Study Showing Brains Differ for Gender Dysphoria Doesn't Prove Transgenderism Innate, Experts Say." Emphasis added.

*Glossary*

1. "Gender," *Merriam Webster Dictionary*, https://www.merriam -webster.com/dictionary/gender.